OUR WILTSHIRE VILLAGE

Steeple Ashton

BETTY SMITH · *Illustrated by* ALAN ANDREW

With best wishes,

Betty Smith

Alan Andrew

ALAN SUTTON
1989

ALAN SUTTON PUBLISHING
BRUNSWICK ROAD · GLOUCESTER

First published 1989

British Library Cataloguing in Publication Data

Smith, Betty Marriott
Our Wiltshire village : Steeple Ashton.
1. Wiltshire Steeple Ashton
I. Title II. Andrew Alan
942.3′15

ISBN 0-86299-700-3

Typesetting and origination by
Alan Sutton Publishing Ltd.
Printed in Great Britain

ACKNOWLEDGEMENTS

I gratefully acknowledge the help and encouragement given to me by many friends, especially Mr Ken Rogers, County Archivist, for his patience and assistance; Dr John Chandler for much good advice; Dr & Mrs Joe Bettey for initial encouragement and Dr David Davies and Miss Rachel Davies for their kindness; my friends Mrs Joan Hanney and particularly Mrs Joan Twiney for proof reading; all the people of the village who have made this book possible; and last but by no means least my husband Ivor, who has patiently supported my efforts.

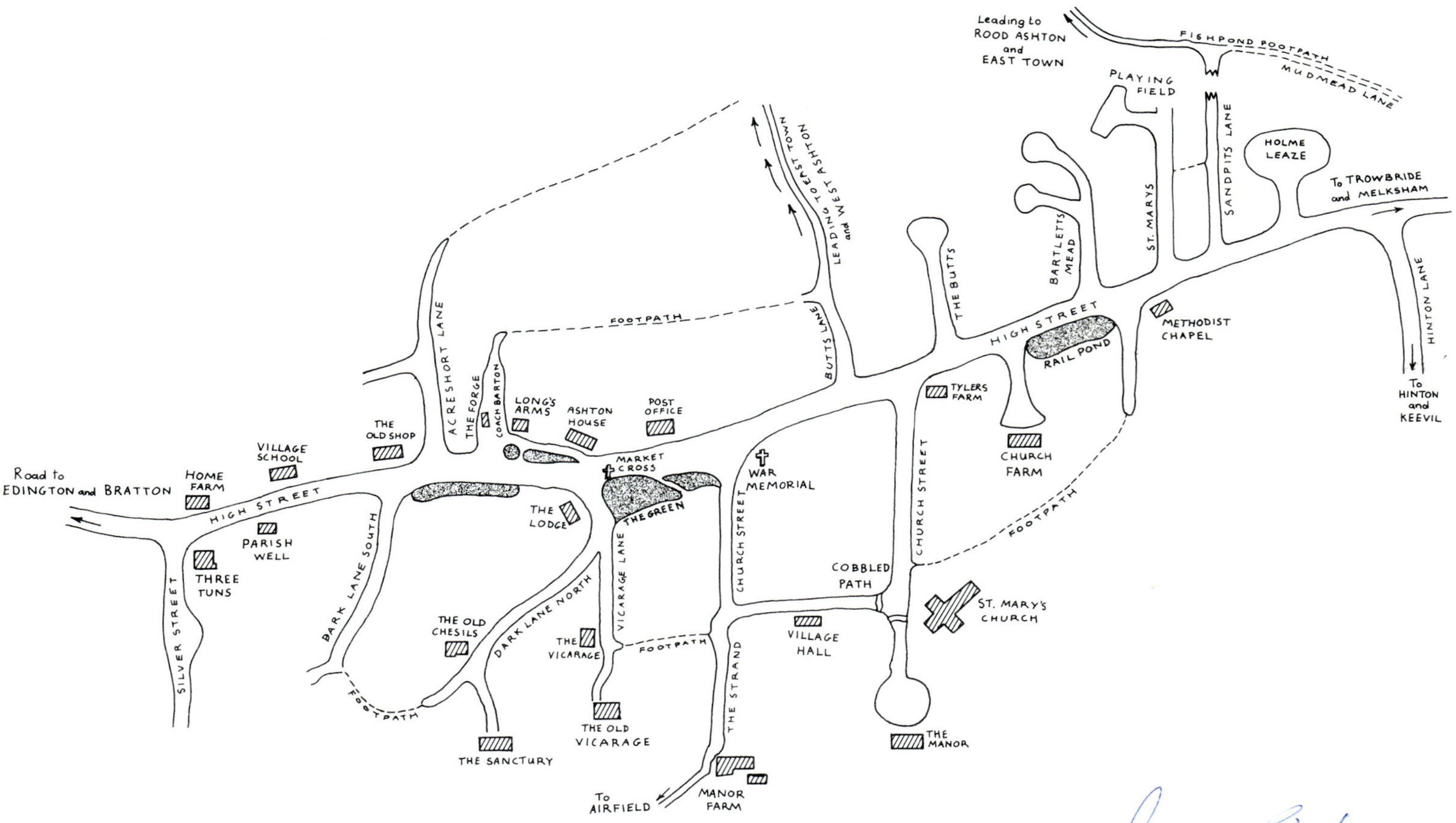

Steeple Ashton

The Village

Where be that blackbird to?
Oi know where 'e be,
'e be in yonder tree, as happy as can be.
For 'e sees oi and oi sees 'e,
Bother oi, 'ouldn't oi swipe 'e?
For if oi 'ad a blinking gurt stick
Bother oi, 'ouldn't oi swipe 'e!
Oi wish oi wur back 'ome in Ayshton
Where all they birds do flock round oi.
Oi'd clap my hands and laugh like billy-oh,
Where all they birds do flock round oi!

So runs the chorus of the polite local version of the Blackbird Song – sung by a Wiltshire man, of course. The last four lines are sung solemnly to the hymn tune, Old Hundredth and hereabouts this old folk song is known as 'The Bradley Anthem' – no one seems to know why. Maybe because it was sung by home-sick young people like the young apprentice Martha Tadd 'aged about twelve years, a poor child of the said Parish' (Steeple Ashton and West Ashton) who was placed 'Apprentice to Thomas Usher of the Parish of North Bradley in the said county [Wiltshire], Yeoman, with him to dwell and serve from the Day and Date of these Presents, until the said Apprentice shall accomplish the full age of twenty-one years . . . During which term the said Apprentice her said Master faithfully shall serve in all lawful business, according to her Power, Wit and Ability; and honestly, orderly and obediently, in all things demean and behave herself towards her said Master and all his during the said term.'

In return Thomas Usher, his Executors and Administrators covenanted with and to the Churchwardens, Overseers, their Executors and Administrators, to instruct the Apprentice 'in the Art and Mystery of Housewifery' and also 'find, provide and allow . . . competent and sufficient Meat, Drink and Apparel, Lodging, Washing and all other things necessary and fit for an Apprentice', ensuring that she should not be in any way a charge upon the said Parish. At the end of the term of apprenticeship she should be provided with 'double apparel of all sorts, good and new (that is to say, a good new suit for the Holy Days, and another for the working days).'

The imposing Indenture was made in the reign of George II on the sixteenth day of January 1758, witnessed by Churchwardens, George Ball, Gent., and James Tily of Steeple Ashton, and Henry Flower of West Ashton, the only Overseer of the Poor, with the consent of Justices of the Peace J. Bythesea and John Madox and signed also by Thomas Usher.

It is possible that this young girl, like many such apprentices, would have thereafter been a very occasional visitor to her family and home. A customary day for such a visit would have been Mid-Lent or Mothering Sunday when, perhaps with other such young people from North Bradley, she would have walked some four miles over field paths and commons to Steeple Ashton, gathering wild flowers, chiefly primroses, along the way for a posy for mother, aunt or grandmother. There would have been an abundance in Biss Wood and along the banks and lanes. Things are quite different today since the use of chemical sprays to control weeds has destroyed many habitats for wild flowers.

It was one of the delights of my childhood in the 1930s to wander the fields and pick primroses and violets to decorate the church for Easter. On Easter Saturday we would take them to church and help to decorate the choir vestry screen, twining ivy and moss around to hide the small shrimp paste pots of water holding the bunches of flowers. There was more moss to hide the small jam jars which contained further bunches of primroses or daffodils. I have a neighbour, now over eighty years young, who still goes for a walk on Good Friday, weather permitting, to gather primroses from a secret place. The

The High Street

cowslips seen in these parts today are to be found on her garden bank and in other private gardens. Once upon a time we would gather them to suck out the sweet nectar as we walked. We also used to make cowslip balls to toss to each other. Some mothers were known to make cowslip wine – not as innocuous as it sounds! In fact very potent!

Young Martha would surely have been welcomed by her family for a meal, possibly some simnel cake, boiled and baked and, if the family were not too poor, decorated with marchpane (marzipan in the modern idiom). The family would by tradition have gone to Mother Church together before Martha made her way back to her master's house before darkness fell.

If she were to return today after some two hundred and thirty years she would still be able to recognize the most photographed view of the village – the High Street from the south, with the old houses standing shoulder to shoulder around the Green with the Market Cross and Blind House and, forming an imposing and satisfying backdrop for the scene, the church. The tall tower and lofty clerestoried nave make it a landmark, visible from many miles. It has been called a miniature or pocket cathedral, even a silver battleship. It is most certainly a majestic church for so small a place.

The present building replaced an earlier one on the same site and that earlier one was most probably a replacement for an older, possibly Saxon, Coople (coupling) Church, which stood half a mile to the east and coupled the parishes of Keevil and Steeple Ashton. For more than four hundred and fifty years the two parishes were separate, each having its own vicar. Steeple Ashton had a Chapel of Ease at St George's, Semington, with a curate from Steeple Ashton and its own Parochial Church Council. In 1972 the Reverend A.R. Moore, Vicar of Steeple Ashton with Semington, was appointed Vicar of Keevil and the two parishes were once again united, but this time each retained its own church and council. One vicar with three parishes.

St Mary's Church in Autumn

The old couple church has never been successfully excavated. During the 1950s the sons of the late Canon O.R. Yerburgh, Vicar from 1932–1958, assisted at a 'dig'. Unfortunately their findings were not up to expectations although they did discover some possible foundations. Mr Ossie Burbidge, a successful local dowser once had his dowsings confirmed as THE SITE, many years ago before the airfield was built.

Steeple Ashton was the principal village of the Manor 'At Aeystone' bequeathed by King Alfred the Great in 899 for the endowment of his youngest daughter Aelfthryth. In due course it was inherited by Alfred's great-grandson, Edgar the Peaceful, the slayer of wolves, who was crowned first King of All England by Dunstan, Archbishop of Canterbury, in the old Saxon Abbey at Bath, which stood in the Orange Grove just east of the present Abbey Church. There is a tablet on the north-east corner of the outer wall recording the crowning on this site on Whit-Sunday in 973 AD.

Like his great-grandsire, Edgar was a wise and prudent man. In the later years of the tenth century men believed that the world might end in the year 1000 AD and deemed it wise to make provision for the safety of their immortal souls – a kind of Eternal Life Assurance! This they hoped to do by donating or bequeathing some of their wealth in cash or kind for the endowment of religious establishments. King Edgar's gift for the endowment of the Nunnery of Romsey, which he re-established in 967, included the Manor At Aeystone with other properties, including nearby Edington (Ethandune). In an imposing charter of 964 he set out its bounds, saying that he should enjoy it for his life-time and leave it to whom he wished.

The Abbess of Romsey was Patron of the Living of Steeple Ashton for most of the time until the Dissolution of the Monasteries by Henry VIII in 1536. A Charter of 1266 granted to the Abbess a weekly market and an annual fair on the Vigil, Feast and Morrow of the Nativity of St Mary (7, 8 and 9 September).

Steeple Ashton was a prosperous little market town in 1420 when the re-building of the old church began. By 1480 the new tower was completed with 'a fayre and lofty spire', admired by John Leland in 1540. The remainder of the church apart from the chancel was rebuilt between 1480 and 1500, the north aisle at the cost of Robert Long and his wife Edith. Most of the cost of the south aisle was borne by Walter Leucas and his wife Maud. The nave was paid for by the parishioners of the time with, it is thought, a little help from Sir Walter Hungerford of Farleigh Castle, Patron from 1490–1509, and the Abbess of Romsey. Robert Long and Walter Leucas were wealthy clothiers until a disastrous fire occurred and according to a court roll of 1503 at least six houses were destroyed and never replaced, many being in the neighbourhood of the church. At the same time there were changes in the woollen industry. Cottage industries were declining and water power was not available. The nearest fulling mill was at Littleton in the parish of Semington. The trade went to Lavington. The clothiers lost money and were unable to pay for the completion of the church building, hence the unfinished carvings, particularly of the roof bosses. The chancel was not replaced until 1853! Nevertheless, the church was dedicated to the Blessed Virgin Mary in September 1500.

Corbel with two right hands

One marvels at the skill of those early builders. There are twenty-two corbels supporting the canopied niches and clerestory pillars. They may well be the likenesses of some of those early masons and other contemporary locals. Each corbel is unique. Some faces are old, some young, some serious, some amusing; hard of hearing, one or two lean with hand cupped to ear towards the preacher, obviously anxious not to miss a single precious word! One has two right hands – a self portrait perhaps? Try to draw your own portrait without benefit of a mirror! Some may portray a wife or lady love, or maybe a mother?

Beneath the niche beside the small south door an angel bears on his shield a memorial brass for Robert Ffoulkes. A lady came from across the ocean a few years ago seeking this memorial to an ancestor! The angel beside the Lady Chapel opposite bears the letter M pierced by a cross. There are four lesser angels, bearing shields and supporting the roof of the Baptistry, the former Beach Chapel, containing many memorials to the Beach family. High on the south wall beneath the angel is a small urn-shaped memorial to seventeen-year-old John Sharp, who died in 1814. We know nothing of him and his untimely death.

However, we do know of the sad, romantic story concealed by the elegant weeping maiden on the white marble memorial on the opposite wall. Ann Wainhouse who is buried in the south aisle fell in love with the curate of Steeple Ashton. Her father opposed her wish to marry this curate, William Wainhouse, and kept her locked up in solitary confinement in her room over the porch at Keevil Manor, attended only by a black servant. After a year, when she had not changed her mind he relented. Ann and William were married and came to Steeple Ashton to live. Some have been heard to say that William was no kinder than her father had been. The marriage was brief. Ann died in February 1771 in her twenty-second year.

Richard Crawley was vicar for forty-one years, 1828–70. He was also the last unmarried vicar for the parish. When his mother, Mary, died in 1841 her sons and daughters gave the new font in her memory. It has a fine oak, crocketed steeple lid, with a heavy counter-balancing weight to raise and lower it. Font lids had been introduced many years before to prevent the water being taken for black magic practices, at a time when such water was blessed when renewed twice a year. The 'holy' water used today comes from the hot tap at 4, Church Street, the home of the last, and the present verger. This font has a plug and a drain. However, it is rarely used now as there is a portable font and baptisms take place in the north cross aisle where it meets the nave.

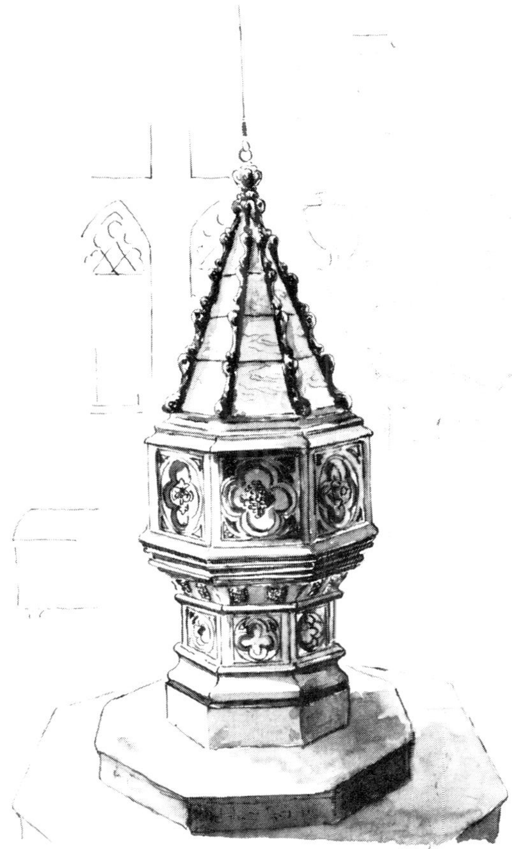

The Font

Long before the days of banks and record offices the church treasures and documents were housed in the early fifteenth-century oak chest with its iron bands and central gothic lock, plate and hasp, which is kept in the Baptistry today. Maybe it was found that some priests and/or churchwardens were not as honest as they should have been because an Act of King Edward VI (1547–53) decreed that such chests should have three locks and in due time our chest had two further locks fitted. The keys were then held by three different persons, usually the vicar and each of the churchwardens. It was necessary for all three to gather together for the opening of the chest. It was unlikely that three such persons would make off together with the money, plate or title deeds, although a single key-holder might have done so in earlier days. We have not heard of any such malpractice in connection with Steeple Ashton.

DESTRUCTION

There was war in England, civil war. Oliver Cromwell and the Roundheads challenged the authority and rule of Charles I and the Divine Right of Kings. There were battles and skirmishes in all parts of the country, including Wiltshire. The Battle of Roundway Down, near Devizes, took place in 1643 and ended with a Royalist victory. Sir William Waller, the defeated Parliamentarian General, returned to the area two years later and met the forces of Sir Robert Long near Melksham. The action was inconclusive but afterwards Sir William Waller and his men came to Steeple Ashton, where they camped in the church. Men brought their horses into church and stabled them in the box pews. They set about demolishing what they called signs of idolatry in the building. They destroyed the stained glass windows but were less successful in destroying the corbels – only one was damaged – the old gentleman beside the great door lost part of his face.

After the departure of their unwelcome guests, the villagers gathered to inspect the damage and do what they could to repair it. They collected many pieces of the beautiful stained glass which were incorporated into the replacement windows. Among the fragments are rayed suns, symbols used by Richard III, the king who lost his crown at Bosworth Field in 1485. Henry of Lancaster recovered that crown from a thorn bush, married Richard's sister, Elizabeth of York, founded the Tudor dynasty and brought peace to England as Henry VII. There are many Tudor Roses in the windows and also some in the roof bosses.

TRAGEDY

There was a violent thunderstorm on 25 July, 1670 – twenty-five years after the sad destruction of the windows. This time the steeple was struck by lightning. The repairs were almost completed – the workmen were about to put in the last stone – when their attention was drawn to a fast-approaching black cloud, sailing towards them. They were advised to make haste and come down from the scaffolding, but before they could do so, the cloud overwhelmed them. There was a violent crack of thunder as lightning struck again. The steeple fell down across the church, causing great damage and the two workmen were killed. Two days later, on 17 October, 1670 they were buried together in a grave in the north aisle near the porch. John Robbins and John Bartlett, the master craftsmen, are commemorated on the brass plate beside the choir vestry which records the incident.

The repairs were completed in 1675 at a cost of four hundred and twenty pounds. Two of the bosses in the south aisle roof bear initials IS and IT for John Stileman and John Tucker, the church wardens named on the brass plate. One of the bosses in the north aisle (built at the cost of Robert Long) shows a 'tun' or barrel with a sprig growing from it. Ash-ton? Some horse brasses used on the Long's estate prior to 1930 are tun shaped.

There are many memorials to the Long family. The west window, depicting ladies of the bible, was given by Richard Walmesley in memory of his wife and her three sisters all daughters of Richard Godolphin Long, in 1879. Perhaps they are shown on the print in the vicar's vestry, dedicated to Walter Long, Esq., MP, by J. Howell of Steeple Ashton, which shows the interior of the

A view of St Mary's Church from the west

church as it was before 1853 when the Patrons, Magdalene College, Cambridge, arranged for the original chancel to be replaced – so sympathetically that it looks as if it were the restored chancel of 1480.

In the Lady Chapel at the east end of the north aisle is the organ given by Catherine Long in memory of her husband Richard Penruddocke Long in 1877. The organ was fitted with an electric blower in thanksgiving for the safe return from the 1939–45 war of the three Tilton sons. The old hand blower, pumped like a blacksmith's bellows, is retained and has been used when the electricity has failed. It was quite hard work, and something of an art, to keep the organ properly supplied with wind, as I know well. On more than one occasion, often on a wash day, I have answered my late father-in-law's SOS and left my housework to blow the organ for a funeral service!

Some of the finest carvings in the roof are hidden by the organ. The Virgin Mary, hands clasped in prayer, and supported by four angels cannot now be readily seen. The very fine carving of the next bay, behind the choir stalls, is clearly visible. it shows our Lord in Glory, an orb in His left hand and His right hand raised in Blessing, surrounded by four prophets and three female figures, throught to be Esther, The Queen of Sheba and St Anne. Perhaps at some future date a new organ will be required and the whole of this beautiful roof may be revealed.

Over the great south door is a memorial to Samuel Hey, vicar of this parish and a renowned preacher, born in Pudsey, the home of the once renowned cricketer Len Hutton, as old cricket lovers will know. Samuel Hey was known as the Hermit, because of his reclusive way of life. He was a good man who cared for his parishioners like a father. He added many books to the small library which he inherited from his predecessors. At his death in 1828 he bequeathed his library and some furniture to his successors. When the modern vicarage was built in 1968 the Parvis or Priest's room over the church porch was converted to a suitable library to contain many of these treasures, including a recently-restored lectern of fruit wood which probably belonged to Samuel Hey.

Other former vicars are remembered in the church. The pulpit is a memorial to Prebendary Crawley and the massive altar of solid oak was presented by Ann Hartley in memory of her husband who was vicar from 1870–89. The painted panels of the reredos had to be removed after being damaged by an unknown vandal. The carving still remains – the top part is in the Hey library. Canon Knubley's memorial is the window in the north wall beside the main altar and his successor Canon Yerburgh is commemorated by a stained glass panel in the west window of the baptistry.

When the Sunday school seats were removed and the present chapel formed in the south aisle the altar table and rail were made and given by the late Brian

Plummer in memory of his father and father-in-law. It is a worthy memorial to Brian himself.

Other memorials are not so obvious or recorded. The lofty nave roof is much admired for its oak and plaster pattern of fan vaulting and the carvings of the pendants which represent, from east to west, four beasts, four cornucopia with beautifully carved angels, four eagles – over the crossing, and four horses heads. Sometimes these can be clearly perceived when the light catches them, but their true beauty needs the help of binoculars to show them well. I can still see in my mind's eye old Mr William Bartlett, a descendant of the ill-fated John struck from the steeple, with his carpenter's tools in his white apron pocket and a diamond-shaped oak block tucked under his left arm as he climbed to the roof by way of three ladders lashed together to make a very, very long one, in order to repair the pillar capital on the north side of the nave near to the choir vestry – a very brave and skilful craftsman. This must have been in 1930 or 1931. It is still a vivid memory.

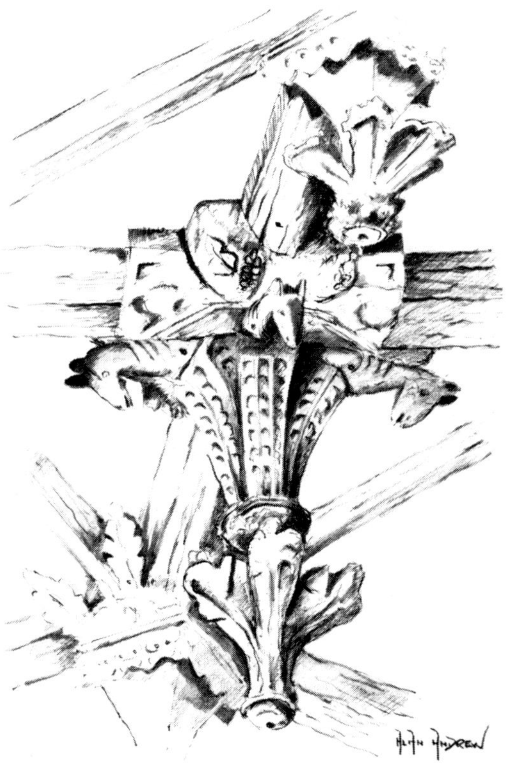

Carvings in the roof of the Nave

The great south door is most probably the original door. It is of double thickness with large studs on the outer side and long, doubled-over blacksmith-made nails on the inside, designed to give protection to those in need of sanctuary in troubled times and to repel intruders. A man who attempted to break down this door would have his shoulders dislocated when his axe encountered these nails. The original key, now removed for safe keeping, was at least fifteen inches long, a bit hefty for a watch chain! Its modern counterpart is six inches long and weighs half a pound! The latched outer doors of oak were restored in 1976 in memory of Herbert Charles Smith, Verger, who died in office in March 1976, aged almost eighty-four years, after thirty-five years as full-time verger and many more previous years as unofficial assistant to his predecessor.

On the evening of his death the 'Passing Bell' was tolled by George Moore, at the request of the then vicar, Revd

A.R. Moore. This ancient custom was revived for this one occasion, having been dropped in 1940, when the ringing of church bells was forbidden – except to warn of enemy invasion. Prior to this date it had been the duty of the sexton cum verger to ring this bell at eight o'clock in the morning, usually to advise the parish of the 'passing over' of one of its members. One toll for each year of the deceased's life, tolled singly for a child, in twos for a woman and in threes for a man. This same bell was also tolled at funerals, often as the coffin was taken from church to grave. This is still done sometimes. Frequently after such sad occasions a muffled peal, full, half or quarter, would be rung at night. This is not such a common occurrence nowadays, but when the ringers gather together after the death of one of their number they stand in silence before ringing a muffled peal. On the death of a royal personage the custom of ringing such a peal is followed countrywide.

Bells ring out more joyfully and often to call to worship, to celebrate a wedding or in time of war a victory and best of all for peace. This has been done for centuries. There were great 'Rejoycing Days' stipulated. Ringers were paid five shillings for ringing on 5 November – to celebrate the saving of Parliament from the Gunpowder Plot, or the escape of Guy Fawkes?

It is obvious from the fretted stonework of the bell chamber that bells have been a feature of the church since its earliest days. The churchwardens' accounts refer to the re-casting of bells from the year 1606. The Sanctus or Priest's bell, referred to as the 'ting-tang' was last re-cast in 1809 by James Wells of Aldbourne, who wrote a note on the back of the bill ending: 'In the hope of the bell pleasing the Revd. Mr Hey & your other inhabitants, I remain with respect, Sir, Your Obl. Svt., James Wells.' We cannot answer for Mr Hey but the inhabitants of today can surely say that the bell pleases still, one hundred and eighty years later. Sadly on Whit-Sunday morning, 1988, at eight o'clock, the clapper fell off, but happily Michael Moore effected a repair within the week and it is now as good as new.

The remaining bells were last re-cast in 1959 to provide a musically perfect peal with a ring of six in the key of E flat. The worm-eaten beams and damaged bells stood beside the church path throughout the summer in silent testimony to the need for the work to be done and the necessary fund-raising for the cost of the repairs. On All Saints Day, 1 November 1959, Canon O.R. Yerburgh returned to his former parish to take part in the special Evensong when the Archdeacon of Wiltshire, the Ven. C.A. Plaxton re-dedicated the bells. There were at least fifty ringers from the diocese to take part in the 'Rejoicing' and bells pealed throughout the evening.

THE CHURCH CLOCK

The clock face on the south side of the tower was the subject of some disapproval and much controversy when a generous parishioner paid for it to be painted blue with gilded hands and figures in the mid 1930s. It was less easily seen than in former days when the hands and figures were black on white and clearly visible to men working in the fields as far away as Raydown on the Edington border. Watches were rare and precious, usually pocket watches, not to be taken out on working days when they could be lost or damaged, even supposing farm labourers could ever enjoy the luxury of a watch. Many working men had only the church clock for their time-keeper! The parishioners 'didn't hold with the new fangled idea – suitable only for town clocks.' Obviously they had never heard of the edict of the reign of King Henry VIII which decreed that church clocks should be painted 'blew and the signs upon them in gilts,' the colours of the holy garments made for Aaron the priest – 'as the Lord commanded Moses' – according to the thirty-ninth chapter of the book of Exodus!

The ancient sun-dial over the south porch needs very little maintenance, it continues, as it always has done, to record only the sunny hours! In actual fact the dialled clock needs much less maintenance than once it did. In the very early days it was simply a striking clock without a dial. The churchwardens' book of 1543 records: 'Itm. In the Tower there are 5 grett belles and one smale bell and a clocke.' The keeping of the clock and bells was important and payments to a man to do this are recorded down through the ages.

One of the duties of the verger earlier this century entailed a climb to the clock tower on alternate nights to negotiate a very 'holey floor' and to wind up the weights on the clock, as in a 'Grandfather' or tall-case clock. This was quite an eerie experience, especially if not done before dusk. My husband and his brother Jim would deputize for their father, the verger. They were neither of them keen so they would toss a coin and the loser had to wind the clock. Sometimes on a Saturday night in the spring and summer evenings our young daughters and I would venture up. However, since 1958 this task has been unnecessary as George Moore repaired the clock and 'supplied it with an electric winding apparatus', for which he was thanked in April 1958. It has kept good time except on rare occasions because of a prolonged power failure. George had a reputation throughout the district for being good with old church clocks – an expert in fact. Aided by his son, Michael, who has replaced his father as Steeple Keeper or Tower Master, he has repaired and often modernized the church clocks of Keevil, Edington, Little Cheverell, Westbury, Winsley, Heytesbury and at Sutton Veny where the clock is not on the church but on the school.

GARGOYLES

Those carved monsters, the gargoyles, decorate the outside of the building, around the top of the tower and above the windows. The large ones deflect the rainwater; like great waterspouts they throw the rain clear of the windows and stonework. As with the corbels, no two are alike. Those on the north side have been badly weathered; some have now almost disappeared but those on the south side are still reasonably good. Gargoyles are usually marvellously ugly in order to frighten away evil spirits. One series is supposed to represent the devil, eyeing up a monk and then devouring him and licking his lips with glee! There are smaller and less fearsome ones decorating the window arches.

'Bearing the burden of the church'

After the church services many people linger in the porch to greet their friends, peruse the notice boards and maybe discuss items of interest among the forthcoming events advertised there. I wonder how many notice what is perhaps the oldest piece of graffiti they have ever seen? Partially hidden by the notice board on the west wall is an early scratching 'Antoni Pashant 1579'. In his book *Warp and Weft*, the Story of the Somerset and Wilts woollen industry, Kenneth Rogers, County Archivist, suggests that this may refer to Anthony Passion, a prosperous leaseholder of Littleton Fulling Mill in the parish of Semington in 1545, or maybe a namesake. I wonder whether the notice board hides further interesting items?

It is doubtful if many people look up to see the carving of the Virgin Mary 'in Glory'. The faces of the surrounding angels have been damaged, unfortunately, whether by erosion or by Waller's men is not known. Looking down from the corners are the faces of four men, generally supposed to represent the four Gospel writers, Matthew, Mark, Luke and John. There is a rhyme which continues, 'Bless the bed that I lie on, Four corners to my bed, Four angels round my head, One to Sing and one to Pray and two to carry my soul away.'

Outside in the churchyard there are many interesting old graves. The old churchyard to the north and east has many table tombs. Some are falling in and one has been used periodically as a fox's lair. We suspect that a fox from here was guilty of a heinous crime some years ago. Our neighbours wondered whatever had got into Ivor that he should throw his dead hens over their wall. Ivor knew nothing about that, but he did know that several of his hens had been taken away; there were feathers everywhere and a number of headless hens in our garden. A fox had visited and got under the hen house, drawing the hens by their feet through the slatted floor. Having eaten his fill Reynard had gone on his way. The hens were collected up and buried. Reynard called again and dug them up. A second time they were buried, more deeply this time. Again Reynard came and dug them up and tossed them about the gardens. Finally the hens were buried six feet down and Reynard was defeated. It was just as well that the cubs grew up and left the churchyard, for the next

'The Listening Corbel'

The Adam and Eve Stone

spring there were sheep in the old churchyard keeping the grass down, for that churchyard was not designed for motor mowers. The newer parts are kept in order by volunteers who mow and tidy on a rota basis throughout the grass-growing months. Time was when the grass in the old churchyard was scythed each summer and made into hay, but there are not many men today who can use a scythe and it is more than one man's work to keep the large area tidy.

Near the small door are a number of similar graves commonly referred to as the soldiers' graves. It seems to be assumed that the soldiers were from Waller's army, perhaps they died of wounds while in our church – perhaps they weren't soldiers' graves at all. I have seen similar ones in the old churchyard at Sutton Veny. Also near that small door there is the 'Adam and Eve' stone, which may have been part of an older market cross or a preacher's stone. Some say that the remaining fragments of the old medieval glass are buried beneath this stone.

At strategic points around the perimeter are floodlights, given in memory of former parishioners, Canon and Mrs Blackmore, in 1975. Canon Blackmore had retired from Belvoir, the home of the Duke of Rutland, a county which was wiped from the map in 1974 when Local Government reforms came to pass.

Was it perhaps the sight of the floodlit building which caused the Poet Laureate John Betjemen to liken this church to a silver battleship? Some people pay to have the floodlights on to celebrate wedding anniversaries or special birthdays, thus providing a treat for everyone.

To see the large congregation converging on the floodlit church on Christmas Eve for the midnight service is a magical, never-to-be forgotten pleasure.

At that service the electric lights are not in full use. The mystery of the occasion is enhanced by the soft glow of the candles in the chandeliers, just as they used to be. Candles are placed on the niches, since the old wooden cross candelabra were removed in 1933. Electricity came to the village in 1932 and was installed in the church in 1933. At a service of inauguration and thanksgiving the vicar, Mr Yerburgh said, 'Let there be light' and magically there was light; young George Moore had operated the switches in the choir vestry. In 1984 the re-wiring of the church was complete and again there was a service of thanksgiving and the vicar, now Mr Derek Burden, said 'Let there be light'; again there was light, switched on by the same George Moore, churchwarden!

Sadly, George is no longer with us and he will be greatly missed. He was a very versatile man and could effect many repairs that prevented minor faults becoming major ones. He was a 'wizard' with bell-ropes, clocks and boilers and with Tom and Chris Noad, whose forte was electricity, would keep a weather eye on things. Tom was the church treasurer and a churchwarden and was proud to show the account books which he had kept meticulously for forty years.

It is hard to realize nowadays that there was a wealth of skill in the men of the village, most of them having learnt their craft in the Estate Yard, working for the Long family. The stone-masons put their craft to good use for the church on many occasions. Tom Hibbert, who used his skill to re-cut the wording of the Market Cross in the 1950s, worked with 'young' Frank May in 1936 to replace the western pinnacle on the nave on the south side. They had to cut and shape the 'crockets' to match the existing ones and they repaired the next two pinnacles on the south side of the nave. They also repaired and replaced the tops of the roofs over the stone staircases, one on the south-west of the Baptistry and the other on the north-west of the vicar's vestry, leading to the leads over the south and north aisles, respectively.

The observant may notice that of the four gilded crosses on the pinnacles of the tower one is different from the rest. The one on the north-east corner was mistakenly put on facing south instead of east when a repair was effected in 1934 – not by the aforementioned team – and there it remains to this day!

Discovering the Village

THE MANOR HOUSE AND FARM

Behind the church, to the north-east, stands the present attractive stone Jacobean Manor House. Dating from about 1647, it replaced an earlier house on the site which had been destroyed by fire. It retains the stone mounting-steps for horsemen beside the garden wall and a prominent feature of the property is the granary which stands on tall stone pillars – 'Staddle stones promoted in elegance'. It is entered from a steep, stone, outer stairway, without a hand-rail. The flagged space beneath has often been used as the 'kitchen' where tea has been served and the cups and dishes washed when the grounds have been used for local fêtes. It has been known to be rather draughty. The granary has also been used to exhibit furniture and woollen goods made by ex-servicemen. Also local history exhibitions have been staged there. Much money has been raised for British Legion and village needs.

Although the house and farm belonged to the Long family since 1799 it was not inhabited by any other member of the family until the first dowager Viscountess, known locally as Lady Doreen, made it her home in the late 1920s. Many local people availed themselves of the invitation to visit the Manor and see the third Viscount and his Viscountess arrayed in the robes they wore to the coronation of Her Majesty Queen Elizabeth II in 1953. Many of the former tenants and employees had enjoyed the wedding breakfast of their daughter, the Hon. Noreen Long when she married Major John Bartholomew in the summer of 1947.

The summer of 1976 saw the fourth Viscount and his wife, with friends and neighbours, taking part in a film about vampires with film star Glynis Johns 'speared with a stake' as a female vampire. The Manor House provided the 'location'. It was filmed by Harlech Television but very few local people were able to see it as it did not appear on our local television screens, more's the pity!

The Church, Manor House and Granary

A view of The Manor House and Granary from the Churchyard

The farm which was sold off had been rented away from the house for some years. The dividing gateways have long since been built into walls and the pond has been filled in. The stable and garage block to the house has been converted into a luxury dwelling. The old farm buildings and large barns remain as part of Church Farm; the stone buildings are very old and it is regretted that the dove-cote on the smaller building next to the bull-house has disappeared, being considered beyond repair in pre-grant days.

The former farm cottages facing the churchyard wall have been enlarged and updated and are now owner-occupied. Parts of their very large gardens have been sold off and are now occupied by modern bungalows which face The

Strand. Since 1985 a very large bungalow has been built in the former garden of 3, Church Street, which stretched almost the length of Church Street, behind the village hall. This too has its entrance in The Strand.

COBBLED FOOTPATHS

In bygone days, before tarmacadam and metalled roads, the cobbled footpaths, more properly called pitch paths because of the way the stones were pitched rather than paved, were very necessary in order to allow people to walk about with reasonably dry feet. Those who had no horse to ride had to travel by 'Shanks's pony', that is to say, walk. Ladies used to wear 'pattens' on their feet to raise them from the mire. Pattens were wooden soles, mounted on oval iron rings, attached to the feet with leather loops, not at all the type of footwear for running in, I would think. They looked rather precarious and could have caused a nasty injury if the wearer caught one foot against the opposite shin, for the irons wore thin and sharp!

Our pitch paths or cobbled footpaths appear to converge at the church gate. From there one proceeds in a direct line to Rood Ashton, over fields called Luffenham and Aybury or Albury, after leaving Butts Lane. At the Rood Ashton end it passes cottages at Heath Hill, known by locals as Ethill. For many years I thought it was called Ethel and could never work out why it should have such a name, then I saw Heath Hill written on a map and all became clear. This path was used frequently by funeral processions, a very long walk for the coffin-bearers and an unhappy journey for the mourners, particularly when it rained. Before the church of St John, West Ashton, was built by the Long family of Rood Ashton in 1846, the churchyard of St Mary, Steeple Ashton, was the burial ground for West Ashton also.

This path was also the route taken by Steeple Ashton folk who worked at Rood Ashton for Squire Long. There is a story told of one of the house servants, known as 'Tin-tack' because of his habit of replying to her Ladyship, 'Yes, m'lady, a tin-tack will soon mend that'. He used to carry an umbrella, in case of rain, of course, but it had another use. His fellow workers suspected what this

Cobbled path from West Ashton

was and on one wet day they prevailed upon him to put up the umbrella to keep off the rain. To their great glee and his greater discomfiture when he did so out fell a shower of goodies from the kitchen. Found out!

To the right of Hinton Lane there is a high bank and beneath the grass lies another cobbled footpath. This was regularly used in times past and it used to be kept in good order, regularly weeded and brushed when the village had its own County Council 'Lengthman' to care for the streets and footpaths.

From the church gate the Church Street cobbled path crosses the road outside the church and again across the bottom of The Strand and continues along Vicarage Lane and round Dark Lane North to the house once called 'Vine Cottage', renamed 'The Sanctuary' around 1932. Much of this path has been covered in recent years and only those in the know remember it as it used to be. A walk down the High Street will reveal the pitch path's route. The setts still border the pavement down to Home Farm or up to Bartlett's Farm.

Our friend Jack is a true son of the soil, with a good command of the Wiltshire dialect as used around Steeple Ashton, and he describes a walk from Steeple Ashton through Heath Hill and East Town thus: 'If theest want a good walk theest want to go down Butts Lane, that'll take thee down to thic littel narrow ground. Go down thic littel narrow ground to the bottom, goo wur th'old sheppis (hut) war, go droo thic shard in the hedge. That'll take thee over the brook. When theest goo over the brook watch theeself, else thee'll goo ass over head into the brook, 'cos twur only one plank wide, mind. The go over little Aybury, up over bid Aybury – used to be a cobbled path but they varmers ploughed it up – that never oughta been. Then that'll take thee up thic narrow track at Hethill – turn left then and go up the hill to East Town Farm, past thic old windermejig (windmill). Vollow the track, that'll take thee past Whitelawn – theest used always to vind mushrooms at Whitelawn – over Pinnocks, where we used to get the moorhen's eggs on the big pond. Then come on up Draw Lane, past Quarrel, then theest vind theeself at whoam!' Not a bad idea for a fine day!

CHURCH STREET

A pencil drawing of the view from the church tower about 1850 shows that many of the houses then were thatched. Most that remain today have been tiled. In Church Street the pair of houses nearest to the church are obviously very old, possibly fifteenth-century, as old maybe as the church itself; certainly no later than the mid-sixteenth century. Timber framed with brick in-fill, one has a very large, outside stone chimney and at the other end its partner has a great brick buttress. Recent renovations revealed an altar-stone, with five crosses on its surface, being used a a mantel-stone in a bedroom. Did this come from the older church? Brickwork on the buttressed end shows the line of the original thatched roof. The front doorsteps are paving stones in the cobbled path. Numerous such paving stones in footpaths indicate where cottages formerly stood. There are two on the path by Moorfield Farmhouse on the opposite side of the road, where a pair of cottages burnt down one Saturday morning in 1926, when many people were away for the day on a 'Chapel Outing'. The thatchers had been at work and some loose straw was blown on to a bucket of hot ashes which flared up and the thatch of the low roof caught alight. The young men of the farm fetched water from the wells in the gardens and many willing helpers appeared to move the furniture and belongings to the village hall, according to custom. Other men valiantly tackled the blaze which was well under control by the time the fire brigade arrived from Trowbridge to draw water from the Manor farm pond, but the cottages were irreparably damaged. Not so the Sunday suit, hanging with freshly ironed shirt behind the bedroom door. This was recovered, still in good order, after the fire had been put out!

No 1 Church Street

The land on which the cottages stood became an extension to the garden of Moorfield Farm. No longer a farm, the house is called Moorfield. It is a dignified house of brick with stone quoins and an eighteenth-century stone shelf porch. Roman tiles replaced the original thatch. Like many others in the village Moorfield Farm was a small-holding. Buildings round the house were cowsheds, pigsties and sheds for carts, hay, implements and a stable. The old dairy has long since been converted into a comfortable sitting room and the cow byre is now a garage. In its farm days, prior to the late 1950s, the cows were housed in winter and walked through the village to pasture during the other seasons. Water was collected from the village well and taken to the fields in churns to fill the troughs – often old bath-tubs! Milking was done by hand, usually by a man in a white coat, who wore his cap back to front and sat on a three-legged stool. The milk was cooled over a corrugated cooler and carried in large buckets from door to door for sale. Measures, hooked over the edge of the buckets, were used to transfer the milk to the housewives' jugs. When this practice was discontinued in 1946 milk bottles appeared on Steeple Ashton's doorsteps for the first time in history.

The neighbours in the twin-gabled house next door were frequently aware of the presence of cows in the shed attached to their wall! Cows have a hefty kick and resent being tied up and they moo quite plaintively. From the inside it appears that this house could have been an early conversion of a stable. The farm end has genuine old beams. However, the Ordnance Survey Map of 1841 shows that this house was much bigger and of a slightly different shape. In the garden are two wells and possibly some foundations of earlier buildings. The old drawing shows it much as it is today, but slightly smaller. It had a tiled roof when Moorfield was thatched. The drawing also shows another thatched cottage, close to the road, in the garden beside the present garage. My father-in-law remembered visiting an old gentleman who lived in this small cottage with its earthen floor. By 1914 both cottage and gentleman were gone.

THE VILLAGE HALL

On the opposite side of the road there stood a pair of similar cottages with earthen floors which were replaced by the village hall in 1899. The hall was built on land given by Squire, the Rt Hon. Walter Long, MP, President of the Board of Agriculture at that time. He later became Lord of the Admiralty in 1919 and the first Viscount Long of Wraxall in 1921. Mr Bosanquet of Ashton

House put up the money – £350 – of which he made a gift of £235. It had a 'Club' or committee room, a billiard room, a skittle alley and a stage in its main hall. In 1975 it was renovated. The corrugated iron outer side walls were replaced with 'stone' and the iron roof was replaced by a plastic material to blend pleasantly with the new walls. The interior was re-arranged and a kitchen, lock-up bar and toilet facilities were built on. The new hall had an inner porch and cloakroom facilities and no billiard room. This present hall is admired by many envious visitors who see the pleasantly curtained windows and the sizeable stage with a battery of spotlights. The history of the building is recorded on a plaque beneath the clock which was presented in memory of Ernest Berrett.

Like the church, the village hall has a large part to play in the life of the community. It is used by almost every organization in the village and is run by a committee which includes representatives from most of these organizations. The Women's Institute, Royal British Legion, Forget-me-nots Club for the over-sixties, Steeple Ashton Dancers, Young Farmers, bingo and whist drive *aficionados*, are today's regulars. From time to time there are further education classes for art, keep-fit, yoga and cookery. Between the wars there were regular classes in dairy work and house-keeping skills for senior schoolgirls. On occasions it has been used as an extra class-room. Mothers and toddlers meet there. Baby clinics, doctors' surgeries, wedding receptions, school treats, birthday parties and many other celebratory parties are all held in the village hall. Fund-raising activities for the maintenance of the hall and for other causes take place here: whist drives, bingo, jumble sales, music halls, silent auctions, coffee mornings with bring and buy and other stalls. It is also a place for serious meetings, annual general meetings, synods, harvest suppers, carol singing evenings, girl guide meetings and meetings with slide shows. The Friends of Steeple Ashton slide shows are very popular. The favourite ones are those showing life as it used to be and the newcomers are highly entertained when the old-timers are induced to add their recollections.

During the war it was the home guard base when watch was kept on the church tower. Fortunately the village suffered no damage – the favourite story of a near miss tells how a returning German plane off-loaded its bombs across the fields near Dunge – the next one would have fallen in the middle of our High Street – weren't we lucky? The ones that fell over the fields fell quite harmlessly, fortunately. In the more peaceful days for us of the latter years of the war the canteen for the forces was run in the hall and was very popular, first with the American Forces and then with the Royal Air Force men and women. These things happened a long time ago!

For quite some time after the war on Saturday evenings it became a cinema, run by Mr Norman Andrews of Trowbridge, whose family also ran The New Kinema in Bythesea Road, Trowbridge. The entrance fee was sixpence – pre-decimal money – the old 'tanner'. Until the days when families had television sets as a matter of course, the cinema was very popular and well attended. In still earlier days there were 'Magic Lantern' shows, often in conjunction with the visits of missionaries. Youngsters of today have more sophisticated tastes!

In December 1936 Mr George Burbidge brought his wireless set into the hall so that all who attended the British Legion Social on that evening could listen to the abdication speech of the uncrowned King Edward VIII. The jollifications ceased, Mr Gumm of Keevil ended his broomstick dancing and all listened intently to this historic speech. There was much talk among the elders but the youngsters took the opportunity of a pause for refreshments – lemonade and cakes.

When Her Majesty Queen Elizabeth II was crowned her loyal subjects of Steeple Ashton gathered in the village hall to watch the service on Chris Noad's television set, specially brought in for the event. Later, as on such previous occasions and jubilees there were tea parties for young and old. The young ones were presented with appropriate commemorative cups or mugs, supplied as a result of voluntary subscriptions to the committees set up by the parish council.

There had been a large congregation at the church to listen to the broadcast of the wedding service of the Duke of Kent and Princess Marina. Wedding guests by proxy!

There are few village events which take place without the

The Southern Approach to Steeple Ashton

Old Mill interior

The cobbled path from West Ashton

A product of Steeple Ashton

use of the village hall. It is automatically reserved as an alternative venue, in case of rain, on fête days. It is no longer obligatory, as in former times, for the vicar to be chairman of the village hall committee, with its secretary, bookings secretary, treasurer – formerly a one man job, supported by members from other organizations. These members take turns to see to the opening and locking up arrangements, since there is no longer a fully-paid caretaker. The cleaners rise early to clean and polish and keep the hall ready for use at all times.

SKITTLES

Steeple Ashton has long been famous for its fine skittle players. The men have been league members for as long as anyone can remember, although they have transferred their 'home ground' to Semington of late, because a bar seems to be an essential part of the proceedings nowadays and Steeple Ashton is not a club with a licence. The ladies teams run quite well on tea and home-produced refreshments! The WI hold many 'friendly evenings' and excel at refreshments, as is to be expected. They are very happy in the village hall alley.

On one memorable occasion in 1931 a skittles match was abandoned when Mr H.C. Smith (Bert the blacksmith) and Mr Edgar Berrett (Blighty) led the team to fight a fire at the Manor, using water from the farm pond. They were complimented on their prompt action by the Trowbridge Fire Brigade, which arrived to complete the mopping-up operations. It was noted by the 'Press' that the butler, Mr Armstrong, arrived from London by train to learn of the disaster and was able to commandeer a car to take him from Trowbridge Station to Steeple Ashton!

THE MAGISTRATES' COURT

Throughout its history the village hall has been the home of the Magistrates of Whorwellsdown Petty Sessions, 'one of the oldest benches in the country', said Chairman of the Bench, Mr A.S.G. Blackmore, JP, when welcoming a new magistrate. 'Judicial proceedings were being carried out here in 1249.' Before the building of the village hall the Bench sat in rooms at the Longs' Arms Inn, formerly the Coach and Horses, in High Street. The story that the famous 'bloody Judge Jefferies' lodged at the Old Merchants' Hall to hold Court is but a fanciful fabrication!

CHURCH STREET SHOPS

The two cottages beside the hall were shops during the early part of the present century. The Holloway family kept a small village store in the larger one nearest to the hall and Mr George Austin kept his butcher's shop in the smaller one with its long, low shop window. The wooden porch at the present time misleads strangers into thinking it is the back-door to its neighbour. In due course the youngest Miss Holloway became Mrs Austin and they moved to the next house in the street, with its rounded porch and stone quoins. This is one of the few houses in the village that has a slate roof, like its neighbour on the corner. For many years the butcher's 'cold store' was the pantry of this little house, which was occupied by an older Miss Holloway and, for a time, another sister.

Mr Austin delivered his meat, house to house, over a large rural area and the high covered cart and the brown horse were familiar in Bratton, Edington, Coulston, Erlestoke, Bulkington, Keevil and Hinton as well as in Steeple Ashton. My brother enjoyed a Saturday trip helping the butcher on his rounds. Eventually Mr Austin took on a young partner, Mr Graham Chappell; the horse and cart were replaced by a van and then for a time a mobile shop until in due course Mr Chappell opened a proper shop in former farm buildings in Butts Lane. Since this business closed in 1986 the ladies of the locality have to go to town to shop or rely on deliveries from another butcher from Hinton and Bradford-on-Avon.

While on his rounds from 1930 onwards Mr Austin met many ex-servicemen and encouraged many to join the British Legion, which was then reviving after almost closing down for lack of members. He was in a very good position to be of great assistance to the benevolent committee. Many hardship cases were discreetly dealt with because of his benign assistance.

Miss Holloway lived and died a Victorian lady. For a time the family shop moved to High Street in the premises occupied by the present Post Office Stores. After the shop days she lived in the aforementioned corner cottage with its front door on Church Street and its yard door in The Strand. She kept herself by dress-making. I was very proud of the pretty summer dresses with matching pants that she made for me when I was not yet ten. The interior of the cottage was a veritable 'Aladdin's Cave' of Victorian treasures. I think I was most fascinated by the glass candlesticks with their pendant drops, reminiscent of the triangular 'Snofruits' we bought from the 'Stop Me and Buy One' Wall's ice-cream man on his tricycle. I think they were more properly termed 'Prisms'. They reflected the light to make rainbows! She had many other interesting items of bric-a-brac and was particularly fond of lustre jugs. Ladies of her era went on working long after the present day retirement age – they had to – even if they were eligible for the 'Lloyd George' old age pension it was very small. It was meant to be an assistance rather than an entire income, which it often had to be.

The late Joyce Grenfell's poem, 'Stately as a Galleon' perfectly described for me the progress of Miss Rose Holloway as she sailed down to catch the bus, her long bustled skirts hiding her buttoned boots. She always wore a mantle and a very large hat and carried her silver-topped umbrella. I was most impressed by this unique lady who died in 1958 at the ripe old age of eighty-seven. We'll never see her like again I'm sure.

Church Street House faces up the road towards the church. Before renovation in the 1970s it was known for many years as 'Rowanbrae', so named by the Scots couple who retired there when the estate was sold. They grew tomatoes in an enormous greenhouse which covered most of the garden. My brother, sister and I loved to go there to buy them for our household, they had such an appetizing aroma. Mrs Bannock did a brisk trade from her side door and both liked to chat with children.

This house is most unusual for Steeple Ashton, not only does it have one of the few slate roofs in the village, it also has a cellar, which unfortunately was subject to flooding after heavy rain. Since the thorough renovation we have heard no more of floods. When the renovation was done it was unfortunate that a tablet over the door, beneath the false window, was obliterated. When the new owners were advised of this they had the date painted in over the window, but they were wrongly advised the date of 1815 (Battle of Waterloo), when in fact the date should have been a year earlier – 1814. Presumably that was the date when an old Tudor house acquired its Georgian front, with parapet. When repairs were required for a back bedroom ceiling in 1985, examination of the roof revealed very old timbers belonging to a much earlier structure. It was then suggested that this might once have been the roof of a hay barn which belonged to the very much older, timbered and once thatched house next door in The Strand.

For many years this house had been the home of Walter Berrett and his family. He was a wheelwright and carpenter whose workshops stood where the house 'Kipscombe' has recently been built. Mr Berrett employed many workmen and cart-wheels were bonded – that is the iron tyres were put on – in the yard which is now 'Kipscombe's' garden, with help from the blacksmith's shop to ensure it was well done.

After Mr Walter Berrett and family came Mr Sam Berrett and family. Their occupancy is well remembered because the son, Edgar, commonly known as 'Blighty', was desperately ill with pneumonia, in the pre-Penicillin days, and absolute quiet was ordered until the crisis was passed. The road was strewn with a thick layer of straw to deaden the sound of passing traffic, mainly horse-drawn carts from the farm at the top of The Strand. There was a happy outcome and 'Our Blighty' still rides his bicycle up The Strand to help on the farm, although long past retirement age!

Crisis in illness and the strawing of the roads was a common occurrence before the advance of medical science and the provision of intensive care units in the larger hospitals. Strawing of the road was last done in the village in the summer of 1929 when the schoolmaster, Capt. F. Thomas died.

LONGS VILLAS, CHURCH STREET

The gabled houses on the right-hand side of the road, going down towards the main road, appear today just as they did on the old drawing of the village from the church tower, with neat, fancy tiles, decorated roof ridges and tall gable ends. I feel they were initially built for some of the higher grade of servants of the Longs' Estate. The design and space in them is superior to most of their cottage neighbours. There are similar ones in the High Street near St Mary's and also in Spiers' Piece Lane. Were they perhaps the model houses of their time?

The one on Church Street corner was occupied for many years by one of the Rood Ashton household staff. Two daughters of this household married two brothers named Prosser. Mr Frank Prosser regularly read the lessons and preached at the church on his frequent visits to the village. He was also an artist who painted many oil colour pictures of the neighbourhood. One of Vine Cottage (later The Sanctuary), pre-1914, shows the house with a thatched roof, just as I first remember it.

Like Miss Holloway, the Raymond's unmarried daughter found life difficult in her old age and to sustain herself she undertook to clean the church and act as caretaker of the village hall. In this latter occupation she was viewed askance by the younger generation, for she sat in at the social evenings and did her best to keep the young from mischief, from her seat by the stove.

After the sale of the Longs' Estate Miss Raymond moved out of the Longs Villas house to make way for the new owner, Mrs Hibbert, a farmer's widow who suffered an accident in earlier years which left her with a dis-jointed hip. She walked with a stick but for many, many years she grew her own vegetables and flowers and was an expert at jam- and cake-making and all handicrafts. She made her own staircarpet which was much admired. A staunch member of the Women's Institute, a committee member from the start in 1916, she undertook the running of what was then called the exchange stall – presumably the equivalent of the modern 'bring and buy'. She was a regular attender at church on Sunday mornings and was always to be found behind a stall at church fêtes which were held in the spacious gardens of the Vicarage. She lived to celebrate her one hundredth birthday in 1969, drinking champagne with her doctor, Laurence Henry.

For a few months, as I remember, the central house was shared by two families. Mrs Thomas and her family moved from the School House after her husband died and was succeeded by my father, John Marriott, in November 1929. Mr and Mrs Fred Matthews and their daughter lived in the other half, before moving to their own house on the Green, after THE SALE. The sale of the Estate early in 1930 caused many changes and removals in and around the village. Mr Matthews was nicknamed 'Meshick' or 'Meyshick' for no apparent reason. He was a carpenter and undertaker who had taken over the business premises and workshops of Mr Walter Berrett. Mrs Matthews was often called upon to sit with, and perform the last cares of, the dying. She was a good and reliable friend to families in distress. Whenever the tap-tap-tap of the hammer was heard on a Sunday morning the neighbours would either say, 'Who is dead?' or more often 'I see old so-and-so has gone then!'

Mrs Matthews was another staunch WI member and when the Institute had lapsed at the end of the war she was one of the enthusiasts who visited all the younger women of the village and encouraged them to join the re-formed Institute in time to claim the funds from the lapsing members. In June 1949 the Steeple Ashton WI held their first proper meeting of the revived Institute. Mrs Matthews and Mrs Sam Berrett were also enthusiastic workers for the benefit of the village. They could be counted upon to assist in house-to-house collections for charities; to collect for the Hospital Contributory Scheme; and to arrange school treats and whist drives.

DISTRICT NURSES

The third house of the block, nearest to the War Memorial, was the home of the district nurses. There were two well-known friends, Nurse Laycock and Nurse Tuck, who were famous for the care of the village people, from birth to death, in the early years of this century. Midwifery was important for the district nurse, for at that time all babies were born at home, in what today would be considered very primitive conditions. In the early days there was no piped water; all had to be fetched from the well, either by pump or by hauling it up in a bucket. When water was first piped, about 1913, one stand-pipe had to serve a number of cottages. Clean water buckets were very important then. Before 1929 there was simply one district nurse cum midwife, who continued to serve the village and district until 1946. In those pre-National Health Service days, prior to July 1948, the district nurses were most important people in their communities, having responsibility for the health of the people and calling in the doctor when necessary. At that time ordinary people were wary of calling such an important person; doctors were considered to be for the rich or the gravely ill. They were to be paid too. Half-a-crown or five shillings was not easily come by for poorer people. However, most country doctors were known

The Village Well

to be kind and to overlook unpaid bills among their poorer patients. Often they were rewarded with gifts of eggs or produce from the patients' gardens. They could live quite cheaply themselves as a result of this unofficial bartering. It was generally understood that the lord or lady of the manor paid well enough to compensate the doctor for his attention to the poorer tenants and employees. It could be true!

Nurses were on call around the clock and did much home nursing as well as the maternity work and casualty duty. The nearest hospital was five long miles away and transport was anything but comfortable or satisfactory, even though 'twas said that a third class ride was better than a first class walk. Who could walk with a broken leg? Nurse toured the district on her bicycle until her later years when the Nursing Association supplied her with a car, better for her and for her patients. At regular intervals she attended the school to assist at medical examinations and, I think, the dentist's visits, and more often on her own to check heads and hands for lice and scabies. This was mainly a matter of routine, as she expected and found very little of either sort of trouble here.

The Nursing Association was responsible for administration. Money was collected from subscribers at the rate of one penny a week for individuals, twopence per week for married couples, with or without young families at home. The nurse in her smart navy blue uniform carried in her bag the essentials for her work, including lint, bandages and cotton wool, which were then much more commonly used than they are today when we have plasters and plastic stitches! Nurse Collyer was our last resident district nurse. The modern system has community nurses and community midwives attached to the surgeries and the doctors send their nurses into the community to minister to the needs of their patients. The earlier nurses had to work with doctors from different surgeries, from Trowbridge, and possibly from Melksham and Westbury, not only in Steeple Ashton but from outlying houses too. Although home births are rare today modern mothers bring their babies home from hospital after a very short stay, some less than a day. The idea of a mother and baby remaining in hospital for a fortnight, as was the case in the 1940s and 1950s, is quite unheard of today! Community nurses attend them in their own homes.

The Hospital Contributory Scheme was run on similar lines to the Nursing Association Scheme, one penny, or fourpence for a family, per week. In each case the collectors gave their services free. However, if the family income exceeded five pounds the hospital treatment had to be paid for directly. The four pence per week was quite a slice of the farm workers' basic wage of thirty-two shillings and sixpence. The schoolmaster earned more than twice as much, five pounds a week and the parson doubled that, one thousand pounds a year in this rich living! How times have changed!

Prudent wage earners could also contribute to a 'Club', such as the Wiltshire Friendly Society; the Wiltshire Working Men's & Women's Conservative Benefit Society, now known as The Holloway Society; the Pioneer Benefit Society, or more locally The Slate Club. On production of a doctor's certificate the 'Club' paid out extra benefits to augment the National Insurance Benefit – then as now contributions were compulsory for wage earners. These benefits were essential when few employers made up the wages for the sick. These societies could also give help with the purchase of glasses or for payment of dentists' bills. For many people the coming of the National Health Service meant compulsory payments rather than optional ones. In this area many of the older people enjoyed many of the new benefits at less cost in the earlier times!

Another sign of the changing times is revealed by the former occupation of the late Mr Elwyn Andrews, who lived in the smaller of the two cottages opposite the War Memorial. For many years he was the envy of many schoolboys because he drove the steam-roller for Messrs Barnes Brothers of Southwick, rolling in the gravel chips when the roads were tarred. Oh for such a luxury today! Like many a motorist I simply hate driving on newly made up roads, with tarred chips flying.

The smell of tar boiling in the old tar barrels was considered to be healthy and was highly recommended as a cure for whooping cough – a disease now rare since the introduction of inoculations.

For many years Mrs Andrews tended the War Memorial. On fine summer evenings these good people could be seen sitting on cushions on the wall about the Memorial knitting, chatting to their friends and enjoying the sunshine and the passing scene. Happy days!

THE WAR MEMORIAL

Erected to the memory of the local men who died in the 1914–18 war and dedicated in 1920, the War Memorial stands as a symbol of sacrifice. Thankfully, far fewer names were added after the 1939–45 war. Each one mourned and lovingly remembered, even after the passing of many years. My generation have poignant memories of our school-fellows, the Sims boys who served in the RAF and whose names face the garden of their former home, which had been the nurses' house.

The number of people with personal recollections of the men who died dwindles year by year, but services of remembrance are held at the War Memorial after the church service each Remembrance Sunday morning, when representatives of the men's branch and women's section of the now Royal British Legion lay poppy wreaths, a very long standing custom. Between the wars remembrance services were held here at 11 o'clock on 11 November, when the two minutes silence was kept. The school-children marched up two by two and were joined by people not away at work. The silence was kept reverently at places of work and in homes. Hooters were sounded to mark the time. All traffic stopped. Nowadays most continues past unabated in speed or sound. Such is freedom so hardly won for us by those who died!

THE STRAND

The cobbled path from Church Street crosses the road and divides Church Street from The Strand; for a time it was cemented over but not too long ago the road was made up over it. However, it remains much as it always was, though a little more worn, in front of the steep-roofed timbered houses beside Church Street House. I think, having lived in the corner end, that this was once a large house, which has been divided up and added to by kitchen quarters at the back. The steep tiled roof clearly shows that it was originally thatched and its timbers suggest a fifteenth- or sixteenth-century origin. The in-filling is of small bricks and only one brick thickness on its sturdy feet of stone. There seems to be a 'mounting stone' on the corner. The corner room was once a saddler's shop and there is a chunk cut from the heavy beam to accommodate a saddle.

Before following the cobbled path round Vicarage Lane to join Dark Lane we should review The Strand. Until 18 October 1963, four cottages stood on the corner, one facing the lane and three facing the road. They were very, very old, timbered and thatched, with low doorways and mullioned windows. Either they had at one time been rather important, or, as was suggested to me many years ago, the mullions had been taken from the church when the old building had been taken down. These cottages were in great need of modernization and too close to the road for comfort. The modern bungalow in their gardens is much more comfortable I'm sure.

The facing cottage is now twice its original size; it has been modernized on more than one occasion during the last sixty years. Mr Victor Rose bought it in 1930, enlarged it and brought it up to date for that era. On Boxing Day morning it was finished, except for the bit of pavement in the front, which he laid before going to church for his wedding that afternoon. That bit of pavement was very necessary. Before the War Department made a good road to give access to the airfield in 1941 crossing The Strand in wet weather was horribly hazardous. It was necessary to hop or jump from tuft of grass to pile of drier mud between the deep rutted cart-tracks, made by the farm wagons en route to the Manor Farm-yard.

This little house had a thatched roof underneath the tiles on the older part until major alterations were made in 1978–9. For many years a tap beside the back gate supplied water for all the houses in The Strand and many of its Church Street neighbours. Before the tap was installed, just before the 1914 war, water was collected from the well behind the Holloway's shop in Church Street. There was a very well-worn path through what is now the dining room of No. 1. Cleanliness comes next to Godliness, the saying goes – it was extremely hard work for our predecessors!

After the coming of the airfield one inconvenience was exchanged for another. The road was made good to facilitate the passing of lorries, large and heavily laden, initially with Spitfire parts and engines, on the way through the farm-yard to the hangar, newly built for assembling the planes. These were then tested on runways at the newly built airfield, which cost us our heritage of many trees and acres of good farm land. The old farm buildings – the large barn with its double doors to the threshing floor; the chimney for the steam engines which replaced the horses that walked round in the apse-ended adjunct, to provide 'horse-power' for threshing machines, chaff-cutters and the like – were surrounded first by men from the United States Air Force and later by men of the Royal Air Force and their aeroplanes and gliders.

Home on leave in September 1944, my husband and I walked up this road and through the farm-yard, astonished to see the fields were covered by gliders. We had never seen any before and the fields were full of wings, as far as we could see. A fantastic sight and most awe-inspiring. A week later we were gone and so were they. They had been towed across the Channel to the battle of Arnhem. Very, very brave men! Later we were told: 'You should have been here to see our church tower like Eros in the middle of Piccadilly Circus, with planes and gliders flying around instead of London buses and taxis!'

It is many years since Spitfires were assembled in the hangar. Since the war it has been used for storage of other aircraft engines, rubber and tyres for the Avon Rubber Company of Melksham, the assembling and packing of DIY furniture and many other things. From time to time this No. 2 Warehouse changes hands and new owners send bigger and heavier lorries up and down our roads to the annoyance and danger of the local people.

In spite of these encroachments Manor Farmyard is still in use. The large herd of cows which occupied the modern milking parlour have gone. They had replaced a smaller herd which had been much more labour intensive, being hand-milked by men in white caps and coats, sitting on the traditional three-legged stools. During the First World War there were milk-maids in attendance on the cows. One of the favourite film shows includes a photograph of Mrs Violet Bull (née Burbidge) in her sunbonnet and apron and carrying her stool. Those days are past. The Common Market calls the tune and beef cattle replaced the milking herds. The bleating of sheep is heard and the little lambs gambol with their mothers where the gliders once parked.

Each May time the tractors go up and down The Strand, all day long until dark, drawing high trailer loads of green grass to be mixed with sickly smelling molasses to make silage which the cattle enjoy. Instead of the old heaps of silage the present method is to store it in large black polythene rolls. These huge black sausages stored outside, end to end, are quite a feature in some parts of the countryside and I would think they make useful windbreaks until they are used. I am pleased to say that in this farm-yard the sweet smell of fragrant hay still assails the nostrils for most of the year.

As we return from the farm-yard we pass the new bungalows, previously mentioned, on the right. The cottage by the farm gate once housed the head milker and next to it is the the old house where Dr Haythornthwaite lived and held a surgery. He once found an entrance to an old tunnel in his garden near its boundary with the former vicarage garden, towards The Sanctuary. He didn't get far along it and sealed it up, recording its presence on the concrete cover. This discovery gave rise to much excitement and was said to lend substance to the fable that there was once a secret passage leading from the church to The Sanctuary. Its eighteenth-century neighbour, a smaller version of the Moorfield Farm House style, has no such fantasy.

Past the new bungalow and round to the left we pick up the cobbled path again and note the small cottage tacked on to the rear of the old saddler's house and the pretty garden alongside the grassy lane. This is half its original length, the post and rails which were placed at the end to prevent the passage of

Manor Farm Buildings

wheeled vehicles – originally horse and cart – have moved northwards to permit the opening in the former vicarage garden wall to provide access for new houses built in the old gardens. The old herbaceous borders have gone but the Lime trees on the lawn still give forth their heady scent, attracting the bees in season.

From the iron gate at the end of the stone wall some of the former vicarage can be seen. The Old Parsonage, nearest the gate, as its name implies, was the first vicarage – a fourteenth-century 'hall' house originally. Its pretty porch was used to house the mowing machines and gardening tools when the vicarage was much larger and included the nineteenth-century extension. This part was divided from the Old Parsonage in the 1970s and re-named Hey House. It has changed hands again and is now named 'Church House', which might be a more appropriate name since the extension was not built in Mr Hey's time but in the time of his successor, Mr Crawley.

This extension was much used by the parish in Revd O.R. Yerburgh's time. The Mothers' Union and Parochial Church Council meetings were held regularly in the drawing room and the adjacent room, which I first knew as Mrs Knubley's bedroom – she was an invalid, was the family billiard room where the scouts and guides met regularly after 1932. Mr Yerburgh founded the 1st Steeple Ashton Scout Troop and his wife founded the 1st Steeple Ashton Company, Girl Guides. On a beautiful sunny, summer evening the whole company were enrolled at a ceremony in the garden. Mrs Yerburgh, Captain, was the first to be enrolled, followed by patrol leaders, seconds and then the remaining guides. I expect the young girl guide who was enrolled on the top of the church tower in 1988 will remember her enrolment as readily as we originals do. I should hope her memory will be as good fifty-five years from now!

These rooms also provided an annexe for the overflow of the garden fêtes – the treasurer's office, in particular. In those far off days the fêtes concluded with dancing on the lawn (the tennis court) if fine. When it was too dark, or wet, the dancing transferred to the village hall. From this lawn a wide path, bordered by flowers and yew hedges, which provided admirable hiding places for children's games, led to the steps, between the Ash trees, straight on towards the fields

The Old Vicarage

towards Keevil, over the deer fence or ha-ha which marked the parish boundary. In the days before the erection of the dividing wall in the garden the spring time view down this path was a very cheering sight. There were wide borders of snowdrops from the lawn to the far garden gate – heavenly!

At the rear of the Old Parsonage is a small granary on proper staddle stones to safeguard formerly the corn and latterly the apples from rats, mice and other hungry creatures.

The coach house of the nineteenth-century became the garage of the twentieth-century and was then converted into a small dwelling house. The potting shed is no longer recognizable since it became 'Stable Cottage'. The fowl run and pig stys of earlier days became an allotment garden for more than thirty years before being added to the next door property. The dividing wall, like the ancient thatched, timbered cottage on the corner, was pulled down and a modern Vicarage was built. Since 1970, like the larger building, this Vicarage provides room for PCC meetings, the modern version of the Sunday school, the Thursday and junior clubs, confirmation classes and Bible study groups, Quest and Lent courses. The mid-week Service of Holy Communion takes place in the Vicarage on Thursday mornings. Ten times a year the Revd and Mrs Burden give up their living rooms for a day for the printing of the Newsletter. This is delivered to each house in the three parishes, giving news of forthcoming events and results and reports of previous happenings, together with a letter from the vicar or guest writer and times of all services for all three churches and the Methodists. For this a voluntary contribution of a pound a year is requested, but it is not obligatory. Wealthier folk often give higher contributions.

The Vicarage is truly a busy place, the hub of the parish, but I feel it is not so convenient for the Vicar and his family as the old building was, in spite of the conveniences and compactness, because it does not allow them nearly as much private space. They really 'live over the shop'.

The well of the demolished cottage can still be found in the corner of the garden. A former inhabitant of this cottage became known as 'Dappy down damson', because of his habit of remarking to passers by 'They damsons, they do dappy down, sno!' (sno is short for thee's know – you know) when the ripe fruit fell on to the footpath, which has disappeared beneath a coat of asphalt hereabouts.

Next to the new Vicarage, round the corner in Dark Lane North is the bungalow, designed by architect and Chairman of the Bench, Mr A.S.G. Blackmore, JP, for his parents who are commemorated by the floodlighting at the church.

The neighbouring renovated cottage was thatched until it lost its roof in a chimney fire of 1970. It might formerly have been described as 'cottage with granny annexe' in the days when it was divided into two. The larger cottage faced towards the church and the one-up one-down cottage stood back to back, facing the other way, both doors being in their respective gardens and not towards the road. For many years members of the Gunstone family lived here, the young family occupying the main cottage with the grandparents living in the smaller one. This small cottage later provided a starter home for many young couples. As late as 1946 there was no piped water or drainage here. Water was collected from a temperamental pump in the larger garden and the dirty water had to be taken across the road to the ditch. No joke for a mother of children!

Fashions change with the years. Once upon a time a large garden, particularly if it had an orchard, was greatly prized. A good husbandman could provide well for his family if he had space to grow vegetables, fruit and some flowers, with further space for hens and ducks underneath the fruit trees. The fashion now is mostly for small ornamental gardens which need little maintenance. Fresh vegetables and fruit are readily obtained. The store cupboard is readily stocked with high quality tinned fruit and vegetables. Time was when food from tins was a source of food poisoning and many older folk refused to buy tinned goods, but matters have greatly improved. Who would have thought of buying tinned new potatoes in pre-war days? They are one of the foods that cannot, as yet, be stored in the deep-freeze unit. The firms that sell frozen vegetables and fruits claim that their products are frozen when at their best and are more wholesome than food that is bought from the shops and not used immediately. They have a point in that argument. A prudent housewife with a good husbandman freezes the surplus produce from their own garden and eats home-grown strawberries and raspberries at Christmas, or even Easter!

Nevertheless the trend for smaller gardens continues and here in Dark Lane where the two small cottages have been transformed into one larger dwelling the surplus garden and orchard has provided space for another bungalow, half-hidden among the trees. It is certainly more pleasant and acceptable to build a bungalow thus than to fill the space with a large house or two, flanked with garages and very little garden area. The neighbouring stone cottage has been renovated and enlarged in recent years. Next to this is the former 'Vine Cottage', now The Sanctuary, probably the oldest house in the village. Built of brick with its well preserved timber framing on view it has a cruck truss retained inside. The long window in the jettied end towards the lane shows where a renovation of 1930–31 had a veranda built over the footpath to the back door. Vine Cottage was the subject of a painting by Mr Frank Prosser in the early part of this century. In the foreground a straw-hatted man in a long white smock with gathered or smocked yoke chats to a lady wearing a smart white blouse and ankle-length blue skirt, of the Edwardian fashion. Perhaps he is on his way back from driving the cows into the field, known as the Orchard, belonging to Vine Cottage and she is the lady of the house, Sarah Jane Moore, née Smith. The roof was neatly thatched then, not tiled as now.

My late mother-in-law declared the place was haunted, but her son Ivor, my husband, thinks she was fooled by the birds and mice or even rats which got into the thatch. It is possible that this was once a moated house. Certainly there was much water surrounding it on the north and east sides, but they may have been fishponds or a water supply for the cows which were kept when it was a small-holding.

There have been many stories connecting this house with the church. No other traces of Dr Haythornthwaite's tunnel have ever been found, so we cannot substantiate the theory that this was a place of sanctuary for monks or priests in troubled times. The question still remains, 'Did mother-in-law really see ghosts?'

Mr Prosser included in the picture the cruck end of the small cottage opposite, known for many years in the past as 'Box Cottage', until a young tenant in 1974 decided to trim the box hedge with a flame thrower – very modern! Unfortunately the thatched roof disappeared along with the hedge and

The Sanctuary, formerly Vine Cottage

the cottage was badly damaged. Every cloud has its silver lining however. The cost of restoring, re-thatching and re-insuring was prohibitively high, but again, renovations permitted alterations and an improved standard of comfort for the owners. Thick, thatched roofs direct rainwater well away from house walls, most important if the walls are of wattle and daub or similar construction, as the stout plinth base suggests this one is. The replacement of thatch with tiles or slates can cause problems when unprotected walls are attacked by driving rain. The end wall of this cottage has a coat of grey 'roughcast' to protect it. I overheard a conversation, many years ago, on the subject of this cottage which had been colour-washed, as was the fashion. The speaker asked: 'Have you seen Jimmy Hindon's cottage lately? He's been and had it whitewashed PINK!'

The cobbled path here is mostly hidden by grass but it can be clearly seen in front of the next cottage as it leaves the cul-de-sac.

GOD'S CORNER – THE CHESILS

This area was known as God's Corner during the nineteenth century, because it was a meeting place for The Church of Jesus Christ of Latter-Day Saints, more commonly called Mormons. Meetings were held in many homes in Steeple Ashton and on the Common, but this seemed to be the chief meeting place.

Cruck-framed cottage, Dark Lane

Meetings were held in the orchard of the Chesils throughout the century. Many Mormons emigrated from this area to the United States of America, making for Salt Lake City, Utah, from 1840 onwards. Many belonged to the Berrett family and one of their descendants, a Mormon Bishop, LaMar Berrett, has written two books on the subject. One volume *Down Berrett Lane* tells of the Steeple Ashton families and traces the family histories, of both those who emigrated and those who stayed behind. The other volume deals with the all-American families. They make fascinating reading.

This old thatched cottage has had a variety of names in past days: Cherry Tree Cottage, Pear Tree Cottage, The Chesils, Chesils and Old Chesils. It has a long history and is probably contemporary with Box Cottage. It is the last remaining thatched cottage in Dark Lane. For many years it was the home of the Sims family, who cultivated its very large garden to good effect. Mr Sims took the produce to Trowbridge market on a flat-bottomed pony cart. In 1932 the cottage was purchased by a lady artist who used its barn as a studio.

'Old Chesils'

Externally the appearance seems hardly to have changed, but of course, internal renovations and improvements have been carried out over the years to make this a pleasantly comfortable home.

PURNELL'S and the BARN

At the turn of the century the Purnell family did most of the threshing of corn for the village, before Mr Cary of Manor Farm started to use a travelling thresher with attendant team. In Purnell's yard stood a stationary steam engine to operate the thresher, attended by a team of men who fed it with stooks of corn. The ears and husks were threshed off and taken along to the winnowing barn next door, where a team of women did the winnowing. This was done in the mid-strey, using double handed leather flaps or flails. A very heavy and dirty job. The women got black in there.

The mid-strey is the area in the centre of the barn having large double doors on opposite sides. They were so designed that ox-carts could go straight through when unloading. Unlike horses oxen cannot go into reverse. At the same time the open doors create a good through-draught to take away the husks, leaving the cleaned grain to be stored in the barn before being ground into flour at the mill. It was some thirty years later that Mrs Gascoyne built in the doorways to convert the barn into her studio.

Miss Sims, from Heath Hill, who had been one of the winnowing women, married Dick Berrett, then a worker in the threshing yard. When the Purnells moved out in 1911 the Berrett family moved into the house. But when the thatch was replaced with tiles two of the gables were taken down. The ungabled part has been a separate cottage since then. Albert Selman repaired the windows in 1910 and signed his name on one of the glass panes, where it remains to this day.

For many years this Mr Berrett worked mainly as a carpenter and wheelwright – taking his wheels to the blacksmith's shop for bonding. His wife and daughters were laundresses – a common occupation for the ladies of the village in the inter-war years. Two large hampers of laundry were collected from Rood Ashton House on Monday mornings. The work was done in the specially provided laundry shed behind the house. All had to be washed, dried, ironed, aired and packed up for return to Rood Ashton House, by horse and cart, on Fridays. In her earlier years Mrs Berrett had walked to Dunge to launder for the Bathard family. There were no Trade Unions then. People were glad to be able to earn money and didn't mind walking miles to keep a good job. Farm workers often walked six miles to work, ready to start at six o'clock in the morning, returning after work ended, about six in the evening. 'Twas all in a day's work to them!

DARK LANE NORTH – FOOTPATH

Beyond the barn the lane narrows to a mere footpath width passing on the right a bungalow, built by Mr Victor Rose who transformed the little house in The Strand. The bungalow stands in the midst of a former paddock, with sheds, where Mr Austin the butcher used to keep his horse and cart. Formerly these buildings had been used as an abattoir by a previous butcher, Mr Marsh. The carcases were taken across the lane to be hung on the beams which now form the car-port for Pear Tree House. The large garden of this house provided room for two bungalows with reasonably sized gardens. They have views clear across the airfield to Bulkington and now that the airfield is not in permanent use their occupants can watch an abundance of wildlife, including deer and foxes, as well as many kinds of birds.

The next two cottages with the ends on to the lane have views towards the hills at Edington. When I first came to the village I liked to accompany Winnie when she collected the milk, from Black Barn Farm, for old Mrs Watts. It took me quite a long time to understand the Wiltshire dialect spoken by Mrs Watts on Friday evenings: 'Here's thee drippence maid'. It had to be explained. Mrs Watts paid three pence to Winnie for collecting the milk each evening.

The narrow footpath truly was always a dark lane. There are no lights along this stretch even today. It made a glorious place for we children to hide when we played 'Fox and Hounds' all round the village on autumn evenings, with many a 'Tally-ho' and 'Halloo-ooo'. We were able to get into the hedges if we were the foxes and then we would double back when the hounds had passed by. Sometimes on a frosty evening we would repair to School House to enjoy some home-made toffee, produced by Mary, who was Mother's help at that time. Happy memories!

There are quite a few bungalows here, on both sides of the lane, all built since 1932. The three much later ones on the left were built in the 1960s on what was once a fine orchard of plums and luscious greengages, as well as apples and pears. Many a hundredweight of fine fruit from here has been sold in Trowbridge Market, at threepence and sixpence a pound. In the early days of the Second World War there were bumper harvests, taken to market by Bert Smith, with his pony and cart. Such fruit was a godsend to add to a war-time diet and was greatly appreciated by the townsfolk. For many years this large garden was cultivated by Bert's father, Granfer William Smith, who had to use a crutch at all times, after breaking his leg by falling from a cart-load of straw. This was a common accident for rural labourers during the early part of this century. He had to be taken to hospital in Bristol for treatment and there he had quite a long stay. His family were greatly relieved when he was brought back to the old Cottage Hospital in The Halve, Trowbridge. The County Council Clinic has stood on that site since 1964. Granfer came home and lived and worked for many years. He died in 1936 at the age of seventy-seven, just short of his seventy-eighth birthday, in Trowbridge Hospital. A local lady who was a nurse at that time told us of Mr Millington – the Music Man – proprietor of The Trowbridge Music Shop of Trowbridge Market Place, known as a 'lay preacher', who regularly visited the Men's Ward at the hospital. He would visit the sick and regularly asked: 'Are you prepared to meet your Maker?' When he came to Granfer he asked the question and received the reply: 'Well, when my son comes in the horse and trap with my clean clothes and my suit, I think I'll be ready to go.'

DARK LANE SOUTH

The lane widens again here and is accessible to motor traffic as far as the entrance to the bungalows' close. There are two bungalows in the former orchard of Old Chesils, where the Mormons used to meet. Because there was insufficient room for lorries to turn round after taking the wrong route, it was decided to name each half of the lane North or South, as appropriate, but naturally the old-timers omit the suffixes.

The small row of old cottages, endwise to the lane, were once the homes of farm workers employed by Brown's of Silver Street. Now converted into one were the two cottages occupied by the Smith family.

In the small central cottage Granfer and his wife Edith Julia had brought up their family of six children, three boys and three girls. In October 1885 William James Smith signed the marriage certificate with a X when he married Edith Julia Mattock of Great Hinton, in St Mary's Church, Steeple Ashton. They had been married for forty-one years when she died after having had two operations for breast cancer. The scrubbed kitchen table of this little house was the operating table on each occasion. Two doctors attended her, one was the surgeon, the other the anaesthetist, both were local GPs. She was nursed by her family and lived for two years after the second mastectomy. Truly, tender, loving care worked wonders in the early 1920s.

I was often told that her children remembered how she used to do the washing for the Stancomb family – important clothiers of Trowbridge. Her youngest son, Bert (Herbert Charles was his baptismal name) would collect and deliver with his pony and trap. Long after his death we learned that the late Mrs Stancomb had mystified her family in her latter years; always on a Tuesday morning she was up bright and early and set off, they didn't know where, until overcome by their curiosity, they kept secret watch and found she was 'hitching a lift' to market with Bert in his pony trap. She must have enjoyed her short trip, she seemed to be a regular customer.

Edith Julia's second son Albert was well known to many in the surrounding villages when he managed the coal business for George of Geo. T. Brown and Son. The job, taken on as a temporary measure, became permanent and grew very difficult during the 1939–45 war. Coal was rationed to one hundredweight per household per week. It was basically fair, sufficient for one fire per household, used mainly in the kitchen where the cooking was done on an open fire or kitchen range. To families in larger houses it caused real hardship. In School House we had been used to using up to five hundredweight of coal each week during the winter months, to heat the large, high rooms. As fires were needed to heat water as well as the house we were glad to have in reserve a Rippingale oil stove with oven and a primus stove to boil a kettle quickly for the early morning cuppa. In our household the potatoes were cooked in a steamer over a pan of boiling water, on the primus. When the potatoes were half-cooked the greens were put into the saucepan for the remaining cooking time. The primus could be turned down so that stews simmered to perfection. One of our childhood treats was a steamed pudding, treacle was my favourite! In fact the primus stove, run on paraffin and pumped to pressure, was the forerunner of the electric boiling ring, and very useful indeed. The Rippingale oven could be very hot, ideal for making scones. Later shortages of coal, sometimes caused by miners' strikes, made unofficial rationing necessary to ensure that the poor and old did not lose out in favour of their more affluent neighbours who, by then, had electric cookers and immersion heaters. Albert was umpire, judge and jury, and truth to tell he subsidized some of the more needy customers in times of hardship. He was a good friend indeed.

The little cottage at the end had a well under its floor. One of its inhabitants was little Mrs 'Liza Lane, who had a parrot, which had to be covered up when the Vicar called. I wonder why? Perhaps it was because there was said to be a sailor relative who taught the parrot!

The long wooden building which runs along behind these cottages, separating them from the Estate-built houses of the 1870s, was the workshop of John Brown and Son, wheelwrights and carpenters. The last wheels produced in Steeple Ashton were made by John and Eddy in the late 1930s. The hub or stock of the wheel was made from a solid block of elm, with a hole cut through the middle to take the axle and holes in the circumference to take the oak spokes which in their turn were inserted into holes in the fellies (felloes – the shaped segments of the circumference of the wheel) generally made of ash. After the parts had been assembled, the wheel was taken to the blacksmith's shop for tyring or bonding.

Bonding was exciting for the onlookers. A telepathy occurred on tyring days, causing boys of all ages from nine to ninety – girls too, to foregather outside the blacksmith's shop to warm themselves by the circular fire made from wood shavings and chippings where the iron hoop was heated. The hoop was made an inch or two shorter than the circumference of the wheel – measured by the 'traveller' a tool on a handle working on the same principle as a mileometer or pedometer. The wooden wheel was fixed on to the bonding platform, a low, circular, iron table on a foot high brick base, then the red hot tyre was lifted with long handled tongs on to the wheel, by three men. It was quickly hammered down into place and immediately doused with buckets of cold water, previously placed in readiness. There was much hissing and rising of steam, the tyre contracted on to the wheel and cooled while the fire was put out and the yard tidied before the wheel was bowled back to the wheelwright's shop for fitting on to the cart or waggon. Another morning's excitement was over and the crowd dispersed.

Mrs Ashby suffered a rather terrifying experience at the shop facing up the lane when, in the summer of 1935 or 6, Mr Perrett of Capp's Lane or The Gated Lane, Heywood, brought his horse to collect a new waggon. The horse was of a rather nervous disposition and didn't seem to appreciate the new waggon. It took fright and bolted down the lane and straight across the road, being brought to a sudden halt when the shafts poked through the shop window. Fortunately no great damage was done and everyone was thankful and relieved that the incident had occurred when it did and not a few minutes later when the school children would have been passing on their way home to lunch.

Tucked into the former garden of Yewden, formerly The Firs and since then Old Firs, is a modern house of the 1980s. It faces towards the Estate-built houses but is discreetly tucked into the old orchard among the trees and does nothing to alter the character of the neighbourhood.

The house, now called Old Firs, is another of the old houses of the village, probably sixteenth-century, similar in style to several others in High Street, having a timber frame on a sturdy stone base, with brick in-filling and a jettied upper storey. When this house underwent repairs in 1931–2 a discrepancy was noted between the measurements of a bedroom and its counterpart below. Investigation revealed a door which had been papered over and behind it a small room. An oriel window was restored. The barge boards over the jettied front were in need of replacement. Mr William Bartlett came and studied the barge boards at School House and then made replacements for the Firs in the same style.

Among the favourite film slides is a picture of a Grant family wedding in this house in Edwardian days. The ladies in their picture hats and beautiful dresses far outdid the flowers in beauty. It was a splendid occasion.

DOWN THE HIGH STREET – LAWN VILLA

On the opposite corner of the lane, on High Street, is a neat Victorian Villa, built, so 'tis said, to house a curate! Over its porch stood a model soldier – actually a door-stop. It was said to be an Irish Fusilier, certainly it was painted in those colours and placed there by retired Fusilier Griffen, maybe a hundred years ago. Someone took it away. The new owners were able to find a copy, though smaller in size, which now stands in the 'blind' window above the door, giving pleasure to many who like the old soldier.

THE BOTTOM SHOP and a WIRELESS CELEBRITY

There used to be three shops, one post office and two public houses in Steeple Ashton High Street, but not any more. There now remain the Longs Arms, and the Post Office Stores. The other shops should not go unrecorded as they were part of the village history for a very long time.

'The Bottom Shop'

The shops were referred to as Top Shop, Middle Shop and Bottom Shop. The Bottom Shop stood in the High Street facing up Dark Lane South. With Middle Shop it claimed to have been the scene of a wool market in medieval times. This one is noticeable for its large external chimney, its many beams and little house porch. For the discerning there is an upstairs window which gives a clear view of the village green. This window was said to be most useful for the people in the room, known as The Counting House, to observe the movements of the market inspector. When he was seen to move away from the Green it was time to tidy up and leave all ready for inspection. That which was not for his eyes but maybe it should have been – was put safely away! So the story goes. . . .

Bread was baked in the oven in the bakehouse at the back here until 1939. Large bundles of wood faggots – best made from hazel branches – were brought in from the garden store, burnt inside the oven and the ash was then brushed out leaving the oven at the correct temperature for the baking of bread, nice crusty cottage loaves. After the bread was taken out on the long wooden paddles, lardy cakes, rich with fat and currants, with a nice syrupy surface, were then put in to bake. Perhaps cakes would be baked for housewives who had no ovens. Not all cottage fires had bake ovens; some used an iron box placed in front of the hot fire, called a Dutch Oven, but not all were even as fortunate as that. They came to the baker to buy the dough and what currants they could afford to make cakes for the baker to cook in his oven. This was quite a common practice. Some lucky families who could afford a joint would bring it to the bakehouse on a Sunday morning to be cooked in time for dinner at twelve.

A favourite dish obtainable from this and other bakeries was 'faggots' sometimes served with peas. The faggots in this case were made from minced pigs' offal, mixed with herbs, formed into balls, wrapped in the caul fat and then cooked. The Holloway family of Church Street, and later Top Shop, were famous for their faggots. Children would be sent with basins to collect them, with a request: 'Plenty of gravy for father, please?' It is thought very likely that the children had their bread dipped in the gravy while father ate most of the faggots.

Mr Victor Ashby, baker and shopkeeper, lived in Bottom Shop with his wife and daughter. Mrs Ashby kept the shop while Victor and daughter Mary went round delivering the bread and groceries during and after the war years. They were welcomed in many houses in the area.

Mr Ashby was interviewed by three programme presenters for the wireless, known these days as radio or even 'tranny' I believe. We all listened avidly, and critically, on each occasion when he was questioned by Alan Gibson, Brandon Acton-Bond or Johnny Morris. He told how he was born in the house and had always lived there. He told stories of the village and its history, saying that it had always been famous for its sheep, pigs and cheese. Sadly cheese making was no longer done in Steeple Ashton in the 1950s. Sheep were no longer a major source of income, but pigs – well they were then plentiful enough, as anyone could tell when the wind blew from the north on a hot summer day! The village had a flourishing pig club, registered with the Ministry of Food in 1948. The pig-keeping members were allowed to buy rations for feeding and were able to keep one half of the fattened pig, but they had to sell the other half to Bowyers of Trowbridge who did the killing and curing. Lucky were the families of the pig-keeping men, especially if the diligent wives could make faggots and chitterlings, that is the cleaned out intestines, plaited and cooked – a great delicacy. Pork pies, liver, kidneys and maybe black puddings made from the blood, appeared on the menu, making a welcome addition for family and friends to the meat rations of early post-war years. The side of bacon hanging in the larder and the ham and forespur on the shelves were more than adequate recompense for the giving up of bacon ration coupons in exchange for pig food coupons.

At the outbreak of war in 1939, Mr Ashby was appointed Food Adviser and put in charge of the emergency rations which were stored at the shop. It was reckoned that in the event of an emergency they could have been distributed in a couple of hours by Mr Ashby, with Mr Lane of Top Shop and the vicar – how long they would have lasted was not estimated, but nine hundredweight of beef, six of baked beans, twenty (one ton) of margarine and two and a half tons of biscuits, to be washed down with one hundredweight of tea, sweetened with six of sugar and two of condensed milk, was not very much for a long siege. After this distribution the shops would have been locked and the remaining provisions would have been accounted for in readiness for further distributions, no doubt. Thankfully it was not put to the test!

Like the pig-keepers, the poultry-keepers gave up their egg ration coupons in exchange for coupons for poultry food. As Mr Ashby said, 'If I had a feather in my tail even I could produce eggs in the spring'. There were always eggs, with some to spare in spring time. Thrifty housewives preserved eggs in isinglass for the winter. They were far superior to the dried-egg rations, but even so there were times when they had a surplus, which could bring in pin-money, if taken to Ashby's shop to be sold to Waldens of Trowbridge. The poultry food, like the pig food, could be stretched by the addition of table scraps and boiled up potatoes as well as the parings of any root vegetables and the hens loved the outside leaves of the cabbages and such. Nothing was wasted.

Ladies and Gentlemen isn't it a sin, to peel a potato and throw away the skin?
For the skin feeds the pigs and the pigs feed you,
Ladies and Gentlemen isn't this true?'

I learnt this little rhyme on my first weekend in Steeple Ashton, from Ivy and Marigold, the two young ladies who worked for Miss Knubley, when our family stayed at the vicarage for our first few days in the village.

With the connivance of the Ashbys we practised thrift in those post-war years, to our mutual advantage, let it be said.

THE ESTATE YARD

The house next to the shop, which now sports lions on the gate-posts, was formerly the home of the estate manager. Here he had his office, from where the work of the Longs Estate was organized. What is now the school playing field was once the wood yard – a fine place for play – where great tree trunks were stored to season. From here they were taken into the workshops, cut up on the circular saw-bench, which was driven by a large stationary steam engine, tended by Mr Ted Burbidge, who blew the whistle to signal time to start or stop work – time to go home from school for dinner, time to start lessons again. There was a large concrete bath filled with creosote into which fence posts, gate posts and such were dipped to make them last. It worked well – fence and gate posts with WHL branded on them can still be found in the fields and lanes. Discarded posts when chopped up make jolly good fire-wood, they give out a good heat, but should not be piled up on the fire or they give out too much heat.

The wood not used for fencing was cut into planks, which stood in the workshops for further seasoning until needed by the carpenters in the shops beyond. The carpenters' workshops had windows looking on to the school playground and, of course, there were many interested onlookers at playtime to watch Mr William Bartlett at work.

After 1930 when Mr Whiting bought the house and workshops the carpenters' shop became the kitchen and dormitories for the Youth Hostels Association's Steeple Ashton Hostel. The men and ladies had separate dormitories and brought their own cotton sleeping bags for use on the bunk beds beneath the Hostel's blankets. Nice, cosy, quilted, zip-up sleeping bags had not then been invented. Conditions were very spartan by today's standards. Most cooked their own meals, but Mrs Whiting, I think, might have cooked for some or at least given assistance, maybe providing some of the food, at a cost. Rules were strict and early in the morning, after cleaning up their quarters, the hikers went off with maps and rucksacks on their backs, stout shoes and strong socks, ladies as well as men wearing khaki shorts. If not at first then certainly in later years came travellers on bicycles though tandems were really the best thing. The ladies on the back were not compelled to pedal as hard as the gentlemen on the front. What a good idea! Sadly the war came and many young people found their fitness and fresh air in other places, at His Majesty's expense, serving their country.

The workshops were then used to store rubber in its raw state, bulky black blocks to be used by the Avon Rubber Company for tyres and many other rubber products, like the dinghies of recent years,.

In the stables Mr Whiting kept horses. The pride of the stable was a great dappled grey Percheron stallion which Mr Whiting walked in the appropriate season, when they visited the mares.

In recent years the house has been renovated and many of the sheds are gone, but the house retains its old beamed back wall and its grand front porch in the original style.

On the opposite side of the road, alongside Lawn Villa, are three pairs of houses. Two matching pairs have stone quoins and pretty porches, the third pair have doors at the side instead of the front. All are set at the top of long gardens. They were built by estate workers for other workers. The matching pairs had housed some of the Home Farm workers. Plaques on the walls show that they were built for WHL – Walter Hume Long – Squire Long, MP and later Viscount Long, in 1877, 1878 and 1901 respectively. The last pair were built for two estate masons who occupied them for the rest of their lives. Mr John Perrett was a staunch churchman, choirman and bell-ringer, well into his old age. Mr Hooper was a very erect man, secretary of the Steeple Ashton Lodge of the Wiltshire Working Men's and Women's Conservative Benefit Society until some time during the Second World War.

These houses had large gardens, back and front. In front they grew potatoes, allowing the wife a small flower border beneath the windows. At the back they grew cabbages and kept hens and pigs. They lived in fine style for their time, although it would have been considered old-fashioned in later years. Waste not, want not, was their motto. They lived up to it. Thrift was a very necessary virtue, for times were hard and there was much unemployment between the wars – a fact often forgotten today. Social Security benefits were minimal; dole money was very low. Those who lived in rural areas and had well tended, large gardens, complete with pig-sty and hen run, were far better fed than their urban counterparts, and they occupied their time to good effect. No one patronized garden centres in those days. Few countrymen bought seeds, they saved them from their own garden and shared them with their neighbours. People who had fruit bushes or orchards were kind to their neighbours; there was always rhubarb in the spring and dandelions for wine-making were free for the picking. The autumn hedges yielded blackberries and the fields produced mushrooms.

THE SCHOOL

It was in the reign of the Stuart King James I that we first hear of a school in Steeple Ashton. The Victoria County History records that the then Vicar, George Webbe, DD (1605–36) is said to have kept a school in the village. In 1779 John Hicks left £5 a year towards paying a schoolmaster to teach poor children. This was first paid to a 'very ingenious and diligent man' who already kept a private school. He was apparently self-educated and taught 'reading, writing arithmetic and mathematics'. In 1808 there were seventy-six children attending day schools in the parish and about one hundred and fifty in 1835. John Togwell bequeathed an annuity of £50 to educate thirty boys and twenty girls in Steeple Ashton and West Ashton in 1815 – when Napoleon met his Waterloo. Unfortunately there was insufficient estate left to meet the charge on his death. The Revd Richard Crawley, MA, Vicar for forty-one years, made his contributions to the school and helped with the cost of clothing the pupils.

The present school was built in about 1839 and affiliated to the National Society by 1846. It is one of the oldest, if not the oldest, schools in Wiltshire. It has been a Church of England School for almost one hundred and fifty years. Thirty or forty girls were taught by a certificated mistress upstairs,while forty boys were taught by an uncertificated master downstairs.

When my father came to the school in 1929 there were one hundred and eight pupils attending in the autumn term but many left at Christmas and numbers have never been so high since. A number of children left at the age of ten and a half or eleven years to attend the high schools in Trowbridge, many gaining free scholarships. All had to cycle to school until the Second World War as there was no early morning bus service. In 1939 Father re-joined the army and was away for three years, leaving Mother with no transport to Staverton where she had been temporary headmistress for almost nine years. The chairman of the school managers, the Revd O.R. Yerburgh, was delighted when she agreed to become permanent headmistress of Steeple Ashton School, where she remained until 1958.

At that time plans were afoot for the reorganization of the education system in the country. All pupils over the age of eleven were to receive secondary school education. Fee paying and scholarship children, that is all who passed the eleven-plus examination, continued to attend the grammar schools; for us that meant the Trowbridge Boys' and the Girls' High Schools. The others attended the secondary modern schools – Nelson Haden Boys or Girls, in Trowbridge after 1941. The secondary modern pupils travelled, free of charge, on special school buses. The high school children had season tickets on the service buses which ran after 1939. This reorganization left far fewer and all younger children to attend the village school. The post-war influx of refugees from Poland, who took over the former RAF camp, swelled the numbers until 1956. For a time a Polish teacher was a very popular member of the staff. Numbers have fluctuated over the years and sometimes there were three teachers, at other times only two. Parents have been encouraged to give voluntary assistance in such things as needlework and crafts and a peripetatic music teacher visits to give lessons. At the present time there are just two teachers, but if the new houses bring families there may have to be an increase again in due course, although many newcomers are better off and send their children to private schools. The younger ones go to Trowbridge and older ones to Dauntseys' at West Lavington, or Stonar, Atworth, instead of the village school or Clarendon Comprehensive, formerly Nelson Haden. The former high schools are now John of Gaunt Comprehensive, serving part of Trowbridge and other rural areas.

The teacher/pupil ratio has changed for the better and the mobile classrooms in the former garden provide superior facilities. The voluntarily-run pre-school play group has its well attended play school in a converted building in the corner of the school playing field – the former wood-yard. Mothers and toddlers have a group which meets in the village hall.

In 1899 the Rt Hon. Walter Hume Long, MP, of Rood Ashton, known locally and affectionately as Squire Long, gave to the parish of Steeple Ashton the present buildings known then as 'The National School and Teacher's House' – 'Such school to be conducted in accordance with the principles of the National Society'.

Four generations of children have passed through the school since then and most of them have happy memories of their schooldays. The children of previous times had more rigid seasons for their play activities than the young ones of today. There was hop-scotch, whip-tops, hoops and skipping, mostly in the spring. Cricket, tip and run, tag and football; scooters, tricycles and bicycles and roller skates came out in turn. There was ice-skating on the lake one very cold winter. The boys would leave early to go to Trowbridge High School so that they had time for a slide on the frozen Paxcroft Brook, whenever it would bear their weight. Not surprisingly they were frequently late for school. Today's children go to school by bus, via West Ashton and Yarnbrook – they often see the deer around Biss Wood, but they don't skate on a frozen stream, which indeed is a very rare sight. We had a craze for yo-yos in 1935, another toy which is seldom seen these days. Skate boards are now the thing and some boys are experts, riding them acrobatically in spectacular fashion. When our daughters went to school hula hoops were the in-thing, very slimming, 'twas said, if you became expert at wiggling the hips to keep the hoop in motion. Fashions in games, like fashions in clothes, hair styles, make-up and habits, come and go, even marbles don't go on for ever, but children have happy times in all ages.

SCHOOL HOUSE AND MEMORIES

The house is possibly as old as the church, like many others in High Street, with its jettied front and carved barge boards – which Mr Bartlett so ably copied for the restoration of The Firs. The stone tiles on the roof are of a prodigious weight and the interior beams, all ancient and genuine, are on show. In our day it was large, draughty and highly inconvenient and in spite of a little modernization I suspect it remains much the same. It needed a great deal of heating and war-time fuel rationing was a penance. From 1929 to 1954 when it was the home of my family it boasted one cold tap in the kitchen. This was an improvement – previously there had been a pump in the yard to supply the sink, and water was drawn up from the well which we found under the coalhouse floor. The discovery was most exciting! My brother, Peter, led the way through the coalhouse to our bicycles and accidentally kicked a piece of coal. There was a splash and a hole appeared before our feet. Father heard our excitement and came hurriedly to the scene to keep us from further exploration and danger. We quickly obeyed him and took our departure for school in Trowbridge. Within a day or so there was a new concrete floor to the School House coalhouse.

As clearly as yesterday I remember our coming to live in Steeple Ashton. It was on a fine sunny Sunday morning in early October 1929 that I first heard of this beautiful village of the West Wiltshire countryside. In accordance with local custom on fine Sunday mornings my father took his children for a long walk while mother prepared the roast beef and Yorkshire pudding, etcetera, for our Sunday lunch. All around the Sheffield parks were other such family groups.

On this particular Sunday we were returning home, down past the lock-up garage, where father kept his car, at the back of our school, Woodseats. Father pushed the pram in which our sister Jean rode in state! My brother and I walked on either side. We were all looking each way to see if it was safe to cross when I remarked upon the uneven pavement, which I thought very dangerous. We crossed in safety and then father told us that country places didn't have pavements, uneven or otherwise. We were thought too young to remember the country lanes round School House, Asterby in Lincolnshire where Peter and I had been born. We had left Asterby after the death of our mother and lived with her sisters in Ecclesall until father had been able to return to Sheffield for more than weekends and holidays. Now, three years, a new mum and a baby sister later, we were told we would move again to live once more in the country. In reply to our excited questions we learnt that the country was a long way down south, called Steeple Ashton near Trowbridge (the Trow rhyming with cow, as is the way with the uninitiated – instead of crow as all locals know).

The previous Sunday's walk had taken us to Hunter's Bar to visit father's old friend, 'Uncle' Billy Bly, who would remove our home to our new address. It was a long way and we would not be able to visit Sheffield very often. Although that made us sad we were eager to see this new abode and could hardly contain our impatience. On the following Sunday we walked again to Ecclesall to bid a sad farewell to our aunts in Blair Atholl Road – that was to be the last of our Sunday morning walks in Sheffield.

Wednesday, 30 October, brought great excitement. 'Uncle' Billy came with his men and the van. When the packing was almost finished Peter and I were allowed to go down to the shop on the corner down at Millhouses. On the way back Peter fell down on the rough path and cut his knee rather badly. I alternately consoled him and urged him up the hill. Mum and Mrs Earnshaw cleaned and bandaged the wound and then we watched the van drive away. It was to be locked into the yard until they were ready to leave about four o'clock next morning. We were assured that the furniture would be unloaded in Steeple Ashton on Friday morning. Because of the hills on the

The Marriott family arrive at the School, 1929

shorter route, which we would take, the van would go by a longer route via the Derby road. Off went the van and in we went to tea with Mrs Earnshaw. This good kind neighbour had reorganized her home so that we could enjoy a comfortable last night in Sheffield, with her, her husband and young son, Gerald – our playmate.

We were up before it was truly light, made our farewells and started on our long journey. We travelled in the Morgan Sports car, two wheels in front, one behind, chain driven as in a motor-cycle, with noise to match. It had a big starting handle – which gave father some exercise. The interior was gloomy because we had the soft hood up to keep out the weather and the small celluloid panel which was the rear window did not admit much light, nor did the removable side panels over the front doors. We were all well wrapped up, but even with rugs over our knees we were not very warm. It was necessary to make fairly frequent stops so that the car engine could be cooled down and the occupants could exercise their limbs and restore circulation! Jean had to be nursed on her mother's lap in order to keep her warm.

At Cirencester we lunched at 'Ann's Pantry' before setting off on the final lap, feeling a mixture of excitement, apprehension and relief. Would we be much longer? What would we find at journey's end? Would we like our new home when we got there?

It was almost half-past three on the afternoon of Thursday, 31 October 1929, when we first saw the name Steeple Ashton on the sign-post at Semington crossroads, long since replaced by the roundabout. 'Not much longer now', said father confidently, 'just over the hill.' We toiled up Hag Hill. Great was the dismay in mother's voice, 'Is this it? Where's the Church? This isn't much of a place!' said she, when we topped the hill and glimpsed a few cottages among the trees. 'Oh no, there is still another hill,' and we chugged up the narrow lane between high banks, topped with tall elm trees, that was Common Hill in those far off days.

We passed the few cottages on the left, the old shed on the right and then the entrance to Loppinger Farm, marked then by two or three tall Poplar trees. Past the signpost at Hinton Lane and then to the corner of the High Street with Sandpits Lane, better known then as Fishponds Lane, where we saw the first house of the village. This was a small thatched farm house, Rose Farm, long since replaced by a bungalow. Beside Rose Farm stood a pair of cottages, which are still there. The one that has recently been extended bore a sign County Police. This was separated from the row of six, fairly new, council houses, now known as St Mary's, by the farm-yard and a gated track and footpath.

There was no footpath alongside the main road beside the tall brick house above a high bank opposite the Methodist chapel and its neighbouring cottages. The pavement started beside the wall of Bartlett's Farm which faced a patch of rough grass under some Withy trees. This was all that was left of 'Rail Pond'. Some battered posts still stood to mark the boundary of the old pond which had been filled in 1922 following the death of young Irene Matthews of Bartlett's Farm, because the pond was held to be the source of the diphtheria infection from which she died. The posts and rails were finally removed in 1933.

In the paddock behind the Withy (Willow) trees stood some old shepherds' huts where the Church Farm chickens lived. Opposite the farm with its tall barn stood a very neat square cottage with its cosy roof of thatch. Church Farm

High Street as seen from the Church Tower

house itself still displayed its jettied upper storey to the right of the front door and beside the thatched summer house on the lawn. Next came Church Street with a fine view of the church between Church Farm and Tyler's Farm, which then had a porched door opening on to the cobbled footpath.

On the opposite side of the road, beside a paddock and orchard, where the entrance to The Butts now is, on the wall of Ball's Farm, facing us as we drove into the village was a large yellow and black AA sign, proudly announcing STEEPLE ASHTON and also informing us that we were ninety-six miles from London! I wonder where that plaque is now? It was taken down at the outbreak of the 1939–45 war, so that no invading enemy should know his whereabouts. Also on that wall were the remains of two large posters, once white, exhorting in very large letters of Conservative blue VOTE FOR LONG. Clearly the exhortation had been obeyed for the Hon. Major Eric Long was the MP for the Westbury Constituency.

So far we had noted the farms and houses but had not seen a solitary person and feeling like intruders in a picture book we looked anxiously around for signs of life. We looked up the road beside the War Memorial and with whoops of joy my brother and I cried, 'Up there – by the railings – there are about six girls and three boys. The girls are skipping with a rope tied to the railings.' In my mind's eye I can picture them still at the bottom of The Strand – 'Salt, pepper, mustard, vinegar . . . .' In a few days I was to know them all.

After stopping by the small green which was then in front of Black Barn Farm, at that time respendent in a glowing coat of Virginia Creeper, we walked the few steps to see the School and School House and quietly returned to the car to drive up to the corner beside the Market Cross and on up towards the Vicarage. The car was parked on the wide grass verge where Merewether's rose-encircled lawn is now. Telling his older children to stay put, speak to no-one and touch nothing, Father took Mother and baby to announce our arrival to the Knubley family in the Vicarage. By the time they reached the front door we had noticed a little, old, bearded gentleman, wearing what we thought was a funny hat – for we had never before noticed a clerical hat with canonical rosette. 'Look at that little old man, do you think he is a tramp?' I asked. No time for an answer, he had poked his head through the window to ask us, 'Are you the Marriott children? Where are your parents? You had better come in, Miss Knubley has your tea ready.' He opened the door and we, rather doubtfully, obeyed him. Before the first introductions were over in the drawing room we found ourselves by a lovely warm fire being offered tea, with a variety of sandwiches, scones and cakes. We were made very welcome. After tea we visited the elderly invalid, Mrs Knubley in her bedroom next door, before being taken under Miss Knubley's care for bath and bed, while mother attended to our little sister. It was all very exciting. Mr Charles Knubley was an expert first aider and he took charge of Peter's injured knee, dressing it daily until it was soundly healed.

Friday, 1 November, All Saints' Day, was a sparkling, never-to-be-forgotten day. As we walked down to the school the grass crunched under our feet and the trees, covered with hoar frost, sparkled and twinkled in the sunshine like fairy Christmas trees. Such days are rare. This one was very special. Father began his duties as Headmaster of Steeple Ashton C of E School – I recently saw his entry in the old School Log Book on the last Open Day. While mother and 'Uncle' Billy with his men were busy we children were taken for a walk round the village by a young lady, named Phyllis, who wore her hair in ringlets, a fascinating style I had not seen before. We met various interested people along the road and were introduced. We called upon her mother, Mrs Austin; I can't quite remember, but I feel sure we had some biscuits there before returning home for lunch. In later years I learnt many fascinating bits of history from Mrs Austin.

Those two days impressed themselves on my memory and I can relive them with pleasure at any time. But please don't ask me what I did last week, it wasn't important.

I remember the gales of that winter, in January 1930 many trees were blown down, just as they were in other parts in the hurricane of October 1987. All the elm trees, and there were many, between Home Farm and Elmsgate fell across the main road. The woodcutters were busy all day trying to clear a way through so that traffic could get to Edington and Bratton. They were not able to clear a way in time for the Sturgess children, Winnie, Cecil and Phyllis, to get to school on time, but they got there – just a little late, after climbing over all the fallen trees which lay in their path. These plucky young people arrived, legs and arms scratched and bleeding, without a murmur. Their journey home was not so arduous.

Later that year I was shown a wren's nest among the roots of one of those fallen trees. I had never seen such a tiny, delicate, structure before. It was my lucky year for we found that a robin had made its nest and laid its eggs on the shelf in the shed at the top of the garden. Living in the country was getting to be very interesting.

There was more to come. During the first few summer holidays in the village we used to play with our friends in the school playground – we were very privileged. One of our favourite games was the kind of cricket, played with a tennis ball, called tip and run. These games were frequently interrupted, not by lost balls, or broken windows, or even arguments about whether one was out or not, but by the sound of the pitter-patter of tiny feet and the baa-ing and bleating of sheep. Down we would rush to the school railings and there we would attempt the impossible task of counting sheep. There must have been thousands of them in flock after flock. On the busiest days the first flock would hardly have disappeared beyond Home Farm corner before another one came into view by the village green. The shepherd with his crook and a dog or two in attendance was taking his flock to Westbury Hill, near to the White Horse and Bratton Castle, for the annual sheep fair. Several flocks a day passed through the village for the best part of a week. Sometimes their arrival was heralded by the sound of sheep bells. This custom was in decline and it is now more than fifty years since sheep passed through this village on the way to Westbury Hill Sheep Fair.

TALES OUT OF SCHOOL

When I visited Mr Fred Berrett to learn the history of Purnells and the winnowing floor, he told me a tale or two about school too.

Down near the brook between Steeple Ashton and Edington there is a field known as Pinnocks, where chestnut trees grew. During the years of the Great War the horse chestnuts, or conkers, were collected by schoolboys and sent off for use in the manufacture of ammunition. I don't think it was a David and Goliath war, either. The conkers were laid to ripen on the floor of the Infants' room. A likely tale, thought I, but that was the story told to, and believed by, the children who collected them.

One fine autumn day, the Headmaster, Mr William Cray, took a class of boys on a conker-collecting expedition. The smallest boy in the class was sent up the tree to shake down the nuts. He could not resist the temptation to take a pot shot at the schoolmaster. He didn't know that he was noticed – nothing was said. They returned to school and Mr Cray, a keen gardener, picked some of the good apples from his trees, cut them into quarters and gave a slice to each boy except one – and he got a flogging!

Whenever the question of school discipline makes headlines in the newspapers I recall the story told by my Mum, which Mr Berrett recounted thus: 'As you know we used to do a lot of painting and decorating for the County Council, mainly in Police Houses and Schools. My brother Jack and I were painting Steeple Ashton school during one summer holiday when Mrs Marriott brought us cups of tea, as she usually did, twice a day. We asked her: "You don't still use the cane do you, Mrs Marriott?" "Not often", she said. "I keep it on top of the cupboard and when the children misbehave I look at them hard, then swivel my eyes to look at the cupboard. They know what is there, so do I. They get the message – that's enough!"

'When my brother Jack met her some three years later he asked: "Have you still got your cane Mrs Marriott?" "It is still there", she replied. "You don't use it very often, do you?" asked Jack. "Oh no," said she, "I told you before, we all know where it is and that is sufficient." Jack laughed. "Next time you go into school you take a look. That cane hasn't been there since last time we painted the school!" I can still hear her chuckle.'

A long time ago, when I was perhaps ten, my father caught one of the boys reading a comic under his desk. 'Is that an interesting paper, my boy?' 'Oh, yes Sir!' said he cheerfully. 'H'm, I used to read books under the desk when I was your age.' 'Oh, Sir!' said the lad all smiles. 'Yes and if you come out here I'll show you what they did to me when they caught me! Hold out your hand.' A stroke of the cane removed the smiles and concentrated the attention on the mental arithmetic test.

Life at school was not all hard work. Many skills were taught in pleasant ways. Boys enjoyed gardening and were able to take home carrots, radishes and lettuces that they had grown. Girls learnt to knit and darn socks – an almost dying art since man-made fibres made for almost indestructable socks. The older girls were delighted to be able to choose the materials, Miss Muffet Prints at four pence three farthings a yard, and make themselves a summer dress. They had a free choice of patterns and colours, but often they chose the same design and material and that year's dressmaking resulted almost in a school uniform for the girls.

It was not called drama, but rehearsals for the school plays and concerts revealed some hidden talents and enhanced the learning. Parents and friends were greatly impressed and supported the concerts which raised extra money for book prizes which were given out at the annual school treat at Christmas time. When further school funds were required there would be a jumble sale. Any other organization in the village could have a jumble sale, but none could match the financial result of the one at school. The school one was always the most profitable and well supported.

Children of more recent years have swimming lessons. Usually they are taken by bus, or perhaps parents' cars, to the swimming pool at Westbury, often accompanied by helpful parents. Swimming lessons were usually part of the curriculum, especially in city schools, but were an un-heard of luxury for country schoolchildren. Pupils of Steeple Ashton have always taken part in the Area and County Schools' Sports, which used to be held on the County Cricket Ground in Trowbridge. All pupils were encouraged to enter for at least one event. The high jump was practised in the school yard with the big door mat to land upon. Rounders was also played on this hard school playground, when it was too wet to go into a field. Now the school has its own field where football and rounders can be played during any season. They have a sand pit for practising the long jump and the field is marked out for a football pitch – no marking goal-posts by putting down the discarded coats for this generation. They have room to spare for practising for their own school sports and the area and county ones. Parents and friends come along to watch and cheer in a way that was not done in our young days. Lucky children!

GALES COTTAGES – HIGH STREET

The larger of these sixteenth-century houses, beyond the school, resembles School House, with its jettied upper storey, barge boards and stone tiled roof.

It too has ancient beams visible in the interior. It has been suggested that the building, which was once three houses and has been reduced to two, was originally one – or a row with the School House forming its other end, before the present school building existed. Perhaps the middle part collapsed or caught fire – we don't know, we haven't sufficient evidence to establish the truth. The houses are a pretty picture since they have been restored and are doubtless far more comfortable. At one time they became almost derelict, a sad picture.

One Saturday afternoon, that I call to mind from about 1933 or 4, smoke was to be seen coming from the centre cottage. In no time at all it seemed a large crowd had gathered. They brought their buckets and quickly organized a chain from the village well, conveniently opposite. Two men manned the well, raising the filled buckets to be passed from hand-to-hand across the road, so that the fire was well under good control by the time the fire engine arrived from Trowbridge. Fires had been fought in this fashion for as long as men could remember.

Old 'Herby' Gale, who lived there, was famous for his pigs. He rejoiced in their value being 'farty a piece' – this saying became a nickname for him. Forty shillings, was at that time two pounds – quite a good price for pigs and his were good quality. He was also a great hoarder, especially of newspapers. The firemen found one bedroom full to capacity with old copies of the local newspaper, *The Wiltshire Times* and most of them had escaped the fire!

The new brick house, with its large garage, next door has a very shady front garden, overshadowed rather by the tall fir trees from the former garden of Home Farm. There used to be a nut hedge here with violets at its feet.

Home Farmhouse is a rambling old building, which has been undergoing renovation since the farm was sold separately. Round the farm-yard are stables and barns. In past days when it was tenanted by one of the Tucker family a large work-force was required to run the farm and many village boys started their working life here, scaring the birds off the crops in the fields. It was often a lonely, scary, job and the children were glad when the weather was kind to them and happier still when they could graduate from the monotonous job to something more interesting with a little responsibility to give them status, even if the hours were longer and the work harder.

Gales Cottages

Peppercorn Cottage

Wild flowers of a village spring

The 'Bottom Shop', Steeple Ashton

The barn at Manor Farm

Granny's Grate

Old Barn interior

In the early days of the twentieth century it is said that almost every farm in and around Steeple Ashton was tenanted by a Mr Tucker. They were renowned for being good tenants and fair masters, farming in the old style, hay, corn and roots; turnips for the sheep and hay for the cows which were milked by hand in the long byre. The milk was used for making butter and cheese. It seemed that all the Tuckers had a reputation for good cheeses. Thatched corn ricks stood in the yards and good hay-stacks in the fields. The little children that spent lonely times in the fields scaring the birds off the seeds joined their families after harvest for gleanings to feed the pigs in cottagers' stys and hens in the garden runs. Some may have found enough to produce a handful or two of flour or make a little wheat wine – whisky's poor relation – but still potent.

The young boys went on to help with the heavy horses, which had to be fed early and late and cleaned and stabled at night. Horses had to be attended to before humans at all times. The reward for helping father with the horses might be a ride on the horse's back at the end of the day – it made a boy feel like a king, monarch of all he surveyed.

Later he might graduate to ploughman, driving these majestic beasts before the plough, keeping the furrows straight and true to sow the seeds in spring or autumn. In the summer there would be the high loads of sweet hay to collect, then corn to be harvested with the reaper and binder and later swedes and mangolds for winter feed. Old fashioned farming was very picturesque to a painter or a non-farm worker, but it was jolly hard and dusty work in the summertime and far from pleasant on a cold winter's day. For the farmer himself there was a little compensation when he rode to hounds and the wily foxes that stole the hens from the farmer's wife's henhouses were hunted over the neighbouring fields and withy beds.

I remember my father being impressed by a young newcomer to the school. Farmer Phillips bought Home Farm and his son John attended the village school. His hobby was, not unnaturally, farming and by the age of ten he had his own pig which he reared successfully. He wasn't greatly interested in some of his school subjects, but relate arithmetic to pig-keeping and John came out top. He wasn't allowed to slack, no-one else took over the care of the pig and later its progeny; it was John's total responsibility. Father thought he would make a good farmer one day. Little did he know how soon that day would come and his prophecy would be fulfilled. Farmer Phillips died young and his son John was farming in earnest for nearly fifty years, adding a good herd of cows and flock of sheep to his fruitful pigs and in the old-fashioned way his wife kept the hens, free-range, of course. After John's death the farm was sold and the house was divided from the farm and the garden provided space for another new house. A new page of history turned.

The field nearest to Home Farm house is known as Conkers, because of the conker (horse-chestnut) trees which have always stood near the entrance. For many years it was commonly used as the village cricket field – in the days when there was a cricket team. Aspiring young cricketers of today have to go to Keevil or Bulkington or to Bratton to play with a non-school team. In the days before there was a school playing field, when father was head, he used to ask a farmer if he had a suitable field where the boys could play football, or where school sports day might be held. Most farmers were only too willing to oblige. Conkers made a very good venue because it was not far from school.

When Farmer John Phillips' daughters were young girl guides the re-formed 1st Steeple Ashton Company of the 1956–66 era enjoyed many a happy evening in this same field, pitching tents, throwing ropes over tree branches, practising camping skills and cooking suppers, which were not always burnt! Sausages and beans were great favourites.

On the wall of the sheds at the farm entrance in pre-war days the second AA Steeple Ashton name-plate marked the end of the village for the motorist.

THE FORMER THREE TUNS

Opposite Home Farm the attractive timbered and thatched cottage with its Tudor chimneys stands at the corner of Silver Street, making an attractive picture at the Edington and Bratton road entrance to the village. To many older inhabitants it is still 'The Three Tuns', although none can recall it as one of the village's many ale-houses, except by repute. At one time it was a rather tumble-down overgrown building, as were many of the thatched cottages,

'The Three Tuns'

before people realised that history was being lost by their disappearance. This cottage was rescued in the 1950s, to make a pleasant home.

SILVER STREET

Silver Street is a short and busy street with very old houses on either side. There is no longer a working farm where once there were two. At the bottom on the right the timbered farm house still stands facing across the fields towards Potterne. Its old cowsheds are mostly stables now. For a time Mr Peter Bowden ran a business there and the racehorses regularly exercised through the village and were shod, of course, by the aptly-named Ivor Smith, the local farrier.

The other farm on the left as you come back to the main road was last farmed by Mr and Mrs Holmes and for many years before that by Mr George Brown. In the Parish Magazine of June 1925 there is an advertisement from: 'Geo. T. Brown, Coal and Coke Merchant, Motor Haulage Contractor, STEEPLE ASHTON, TROWBRIDGE. Petrol supplied from the Pump.' This business was started by using horses and carts instead of the motor lorries, hay and not petrol, by George Brown's father, Alfred. The firm took on the name of Geo. T. Brown in 1919 when the first lorries were acquired. A second advertisement in the same magazine was from Mr Brown's neighbour: 'W.R. & G. GRANT, Hay, Straw, Corn and Coal Merchants, Steeple Ashton, Trowbridge.' Some ten years later Mr George Brown, Chairman of the Parish Council in King George V's Silver Jubilee Year, 1935, acquired the Grant Business and yard, which is now managed by grandson Tim. The old time business employed many carters to carry supplies of hay and straw on horse-drawn wagons over the old coach road on Salisbury Plain to Lavington, Gore's Cross, Tilshead and Shrewton. Often they had to sleep away from home and collect loads to bring back to Steeple Ashton, just as the modern lorry drivers do on deliveries of all kinds to all parts of the country. They don't haul milk now but often carry Usher's ales and beers. I have met these in all parts of the country from Devonshire to Yorkshire.

THE EDINGTON AND BRATTON ROAD – KEEVIL AIRFIELD

Through the centre of the village the old cobbled paths have been paved retaining the border of pitch stones. This pavement ends at Home Farm. Across the road is a footpath leading to Elmsgate – reputed to have been a gateway to the Selwood Forest which covered a vast area into Somerset. The house is often referred to as the red house because of its high brick wall and the tall red brick tower which was added to the much older house for Mr Cary who retired from Manor Farm about the time of the Great War. For a time the gardens were managed as a market garden, later boarding kennels for cats and dogs were established there and a poultry unit occupies the field beyond. There is another poultry concern in the right-hand of the two lanes which meet the main road outside Elmsgate House gate.

The left-hand lane leads to Spiers' Piece Farm and to the right before the farm it branches to Keeper's Cottage and an old windmill, while to the left it leads on to the Keevil Airfield and a path around the perimeter continues to Ashton Mill – once a prosperous farm with its own mill-pond. The farm house was demolished and many of the bricks re-used to build the cottages in High Street, known as Church View. The small mill-pond was a pleasant place for the children of the 1930s to bathe. Much of the land belonging to Spiers' Piece Farm, together with some from Church and Manor farms and some from Keevil, was taken over under a compulsory purchase order in about 1939, for the building of the airfield; the village was invaded by engineers and construction workers, many of them Irishmen. The winter was very wet and then became exceptionally cold – icicles formed on the trees and quite small twigs were coated with a thick layer of ice, causing many to break. It was difficult to walk and impossible to cycle on the roads for a time during January 1940. Life must have been hard for the builders of the airfield living in the newly-erected hutments while preparing the runways.

By 1942 the work was completed. The surrounding roads lost their coating of yellow, clayey mud, the peaceful lanes were no longer quagmires, they had been made into proper roadways. The landscape was changed for ever. Before this the view from the Church Tower had appeared to be a vast forest because of the many trees in the hedgerows surrounding the small fields but now the trees were gone, the hedges were gone, the small fields had become one vast airfield criss-crossed by concrete runways, with a concrete perimeter road and numerous concrete standings for airplanes. In place of the Irish navvies were smart American Air Force men who soon became familiar faces in the village, accepting hospitality from the local girls when not on duty and flying over Europe. Inevitably some fell in love and the girls became GI Brides. I know of only one from Steeple Ashton but there were more from Trowbridge who went to live in America after the war ended.

When the Americans went back home the Royal Air Force men came into

Keevil, many of them young men doing 'National Service', and stayed only a short time. By mid-1948 the camp was empty of service personnel, but was almost immediately occupied by Polish refugees. The German prisoners of war who occupied the huts in Spiers' Piece Lane had been repatriated in 1947.

The contingent of some five hundred Polish people arrived. They were pitifully poor and wasted after years of walking across Europe as refugees from the Russians and the Germans, hiding from enemy forces and being bombed by forces of friends and foes alike. Families were broken up and many lost. They endured appalling hardships during their long travels. There were many teenage boys separated from their families. These boys escaped together fending for themselves as best they could. All found succour at Keevil Camp.

When they first came to the camp they lived communally until they could speak sufficient English to enable them to fend for themselves. The Polish priest took over the RAF Chapel as a Polish Church. He and some of the better educated people helped the rest to learn our language and to integrate into the local community. Officials from the Assistance Board helped in every way possible and gradually these poor people regained their strength and confidence and the community began to prosper as these hard-working fugitives found work in the Trowbridge factories and local farms. The local inhabitants began to complain and ask for extra transport as the buses were already overloaded by the time they got to the village and local people had to make other arrangements for getting to work!

An Anglo-Polish Society was formed and many friendships ensued. The children and a Polish lady teacher attended the village school and some children passed the eleven-plus examination and went on to attend high school.

Goodness alone knows how they managed it but in due time the Polish people attired in their national costumes began to appear at local functions to perform their lively and exciting Polish dances. Indeed this custom has continued until the present day and the modern children dress up and are taught their own country's dances. Polish singers and dancers are welcome everywhere in the neighbourhood and especially at Steeple Ashton.

A few people lived in the village for a while but gradually they bought homes in Trowbridge, initially living two families or more together – maybe three generations. Keevil was empty again. The Polish people were no longer refugees. They had their own church and hall in Trowbridge where they kept alive their Polish traditions. Many became Naturalized Britishers but still retained their own customs.

For many, many years one old lady lived alone at Ashton Mill, independently refusing to move in with her son in Trowbridge. She could speak little, if any, English, but was a familiar sight in the village when she came up to do her shopping. However, the men from Manor Farm advised her regular WRVS visitor, Mrs Betty Bruges MBE, that the old lady was far from well and eventually she was persuaded to move to her son's home to be looked after. Many were sad to know that she had gone.

The Polish people had just left when, in 1956, there was an uprising in Hungary and once again the camp was used for refugees. There were fewer Hungarians than there had been Poles and they made far less impact in the village. Some were fortunate to find work in Trowbridge where they soon went to live. Others were able to contact relatives in other parts of the country and moved to homes elsewhere.

The outlying WAAF and Airmen's quarters in the neighbourhood of Drove Lane, The Tynings on the Edington and Bratton Road on the village side of the brook and others at Lime Kiln Field and in Acreshort Lane were taken over by the Warminster and Westbury Rural District Council as temporary council houses to provide homes for returning ex-servicemen and their families from the village and rural district in 1946. These buildings remained in use for a few years until new houses were built throughout the district. Most of these buildings have long since disappeared and the land has been returned to farm land. A few of the larger buldings, the RAF and later Polish Church and gymnasium is now a barn with a few other farm storage buildings beside it opposite Elmsgate House.

There are still a couple of hangars on the 'drome, used for storage near to Spiers' Piece farm. The control tower is used as the Headquarters of the Bath Gliding Club, which meets on suitable occasions. The wind sock still flies for the assistance of the Gliding Club and the RAF and others who use the airfield for practice and exercises. The local inhabitants are accustomed to being buzzed by low-flying Hercules aircraft from Lyneham dropping parachutes supporting equipment of all shapes and sizes with very pretty parachutes floating lazily down on to the runways. Sometimes a helicopter arrives to drop men for exercises. Somehow the weather often seems to turn nasty and rough when the Army Exercises take place. I feel sorry for these young men who have to spend the night under canvas when it blows a gale and rains for hours or when it is cold and frosty. The weather usually improves and these tough troops leave on a bright and sunny morning. We watched the Hercules refuelling from the flying petrol tankers with their long snouts at the time of the Falklands war in 1982, training over Keevil Airfield.

The Model Aircraft Club, consisting of boys of all ages from seven to seventy plus, meets here and the air is filled with the buzzing of these quite powerful models.

Once or twice a year the RAF hold motor-cycle race meetings. Morning practices are stopped during the times of the local church services. The youngsters of the village take their fathers to watch. They also take time off to watch the vigilant police force stopping the hasty drivers for speeding through the village's 30 mph limit zone – all good for the rates!

The latest Ferrari cars have met for speed trials and club meetings. The Airfield known as Keevil is still a busy place. The Devizes and District PHAB Club organize an annual half-marathon for the physically handicapped and able bodied and other charity funds. They are well supported too.

CHANGING TIMES – FLYING

Aeroplanes were novelties hereabouts before the outbreak of war in 1939. After 1942 they became very much part of life and we have watched many important events since the American Air Force first operated from the airfield and then the gliders left for Arnhem. It has not been an occupied base since 1947 but the runways have been maintained and used for practice, first by RAF Hullavington and later by RAF Lyneham. The Hercules from Lyneham were used during the Falklands campaign and have also dropped supplies to the famine areas of Africa after practising techniques in full view of many of the people of Steeple Ashton, who have had a grandstand view from their homes. It is good for trade when important exercises are staged on the 'drome.

As children we would crane our necks to spot the aeroplanes that flew over our skies and as adults we were thrilled if Concorde could be seen! Between the years 1920 and 1935 some planes landed and could be seen at close quarters. Too close for Mr Walter Berrett's dog, Smoker, which went to East Town with his master and friends to see a plane that had come down. Smoker did not see the propeller in action – it cut off his nose, poor thing!

The first plane that caused excitement came down in the field called Close and in attempting to take off it crashed into a high hedge and plane and pilot were compelled to stay the night. There was more excitement when Sir Alan Cobham's Flying Circus came to Lime Kiln Field; it must have been in 1933 or 4. Flights over the area were offered at half-a-crown a time. Two young men paid their five shillings for a 'flip', but on landing they were heard to remark that they hadn't had much for their money. The pilot then invited them to get back in and he took them up to loop the loop, without any safety belts! Somewhat shaken one declared, on their return, that he had been able to tell the time by Ashton Church Clock when he was upside down. He was a good sport!

By arrangement with the Bath Gliding Club a young gentleman of my acquaintance was treated to a trip in a glider to celebrate his sixteenth birthday. He declared it was 'super' but he hadn't noticed the church clock.

Whenever the weather is suitable and the airfield is free from use by the Services, gliders may be seen floating over quite a wide area as long as daylight lasts. They have quite a soothing sound when they pass overhead.

Balloonists from Bristol and Bath Balloon Festivals often float this way and we hear the burn as they raise power. Once or twice they have been seen to come down on to the airfield before rising up, up and away on their journeys to who knows where.

These pleasant activities add colour to the scene and we all hope that they may continue and never be curtailed by the return of the airfield to active service. We all hope for a peaceful future for this pleasant place and for the world.

SOUTHBROOK LANE

The lane beside Elmsgate House is known as Southbrook. Between it and Spiers' Piece Lane is a small triangle of land, formerly allotment gardens, where now three bungalows are almost hidden behind high hedges. Southbrook Lane has a couple of post-war bungalows and a poultry unit before it winds its way through farm gates to meet the Edington road, past New Grounds Farm, almost opposite to Edington's Ivy Mill with its large mill pond. Merely a lane today, this was once the usual route to Edington and beyond. It was much more important and was the favoured way for the pony and trap journey to Edington station en route for London.

LIME KILN

The Edington and Bratton road continues downhill from Elmsgate and passes the now-extinct track into the field where a lime kiln was once worked. This field was once extensively quarried for stone to be burnt into lime. The Revd Richard Crawley reported that he was shown skeletons, buried no more than two feet beneath the surface, without coffins, clothing or artefacts, other than flints foreign to the soil here. The Hon. Curator of the Wiltshire Archaeological Museum, Captain B. Howard Cunningham, F.S.A. Scot., wrote to say that he and his wife were of the opinion that the interments belonged to the Bronze Age 1600–500 BC, probably early in that period. The flints were thought to be a hammer stone and a scraper. These are the oldest finds known in this parish.

During its working life many tramps died when sheltering from the cold winds beside the warm kiln. They were overcome by the carbon dioxide fumes wafting down from the chimney. Our first chemistry lesson. As children we were advised of this, although the lime kiln had ceased to function and had been used as a rubbish dump since 1932.

It was 1936 before Steeple Ashton had a refuse collection and that was not a weekly one as it is today. Tins, which were not universally used then, together with glass and ashes, had to be buried in the gardens. The ashes and night-soil which had to be buried lightened the clay soil and made for good drainage.

DROVE LANE

The lane to the right, properly called Drove Lane but often referred to as Draw Lane, was possibly part of an old coach road. It connects the main road by a rough track now to East Town. The WAAF quarters and the hospital, in the field called Whitelawn once famous for its mushrooms, have long since been replaced by fields where sheep may safely graze again. Linhams of Westbury have an abattoir on this lane and meat lorries come and go.

There is a small crossroads in the lanes, left leads to East Town Farm fields, forward is the old road to East Town and right leads up to Acreshort Lane at the other end of the Lime Kiln Field. From here there is a good view to Trowbridge or back towards the Bratton Hills and Bratton Castle near to the Westbury White Horse, said to commemorate the Battle of Ethandune. It is pleasant to walk along this lane often accompanied by finches or yellow hammers and other small birds who seem to form a guard of honour on either side and delight in a game like leapfrog. All rise and chirrup and then drop down into the hedges, the one nearest the walker rises and then like a relay race the next one and then the next and the bird from the back reaches the front and drops down as the front one rises. I have noticed this happens in Sandpits or Fishponds Lane and in Butts Lane and oddly enough when the walker turns to retrace steps homewards the birds do likewise! The lane continues past post-war bungalows and a few houses, past the new school playing field to the High Street.

RETURN TO THE HIGH STREET

Acreshort Lane emerges on to the High Street between the bottom shop, with its ring for tying up horses still on the wall, beside the old bakehouse and the listed black wooden barn with its heavy stone tiled roof. The cow yard has been replaced by a useful drive and very pleasant garden, complete with 'heron' to guard the fish pond. The real heron has visited too often in the past – it has a taste for goldfish in garden ponds. The cow byres and cartsheds have gone but the old house looks much as it always did, solid stone front with stone canopied porch and well timbered behind, another example of a new face on a very old building. When it was a farmhouse the Matthews family were famous for their cheeses; there were as many as eighty stored in the loft, to be taken to Trowbridge by horse and cart after dealers had been to buy them. Butter was made here too and sold for sixpence a pound. As late as 1955 the whey breaker, vats and cheese press could be found in the farmhouse along with the milk cooler. From the road outside one can obtain what is probably the most photographed view of the village with the church in the background.

COACH BARTON

The telephone kiosk stands against the side wall in Coach Barton Lane near to the bonding wheel outside the blacksmith's shop, where the anvil still rings with the clout of the hammer. In earlier days a grindstone stood here too and folks brought knives, scissors and chisels for sharpening. Inside the forge the old hand bellows are still used to blow up the fire – the boss says they give better control of the heat and there is less likelihood of burning the iron for the horseshoes, which are bought now pre-formed but still have to be fired and made to fit. A few horses still come for hot shoeing but mostly the smith prepares the shoes here and takes them to the horse to be shod in its own stable or field. There are still old shoes hanging on nails on the wall that were made by Bert Smith many years ago. For many years there was a pencilled note high on the wall, record a gypsy's debt of half-a-crown which he refused to pay. When Bert heard of the man's death he thought he had said good-bye to his money but one day the old gypsy's sons appeared to pay the debt and ask for the note to be rubbed out!

The coach barton was originally the yard where horse-drawn coaches unloaded, the hardy travellers entering the Coach and Horses, now the Long's Arms Inn, for warmth and refreshment, the horses going through the archway to be unhitched and stabled while the coachman and grooms retired to the stable boys' bothy beside the archway. When horse-drawn coaches ceased to travel, in the latter days of the nineteenth century, the archway was blocked off and the bothy became a cottage on the narrow lane that once led to Mr Turner's market garden and cottage. Many fresh vegetables were grown in Steeple Ashton to be taken by horse and cart to Trowbridge Market or shops. This cottage has been considerably enlarged and joined by two neighbours on the bothy side of the lane.

Here the lane shrinks to a footpath, running roughly parallel to the High Street, passing behind Ashton House gardens and alongside the Meads, the once well-tended water meadows. Deep wide ditches were maintained between small fields. In due season the water rose in the ditches which were dammed off to drown the fields in order to stimulate the early growth of grass. This is another skilled art which ceased hereabouts in the late 1930s.

The footpath was put in order by members of the Shaw Trust in 1986. The Shaw Trust is a voluntary organization set up to help small businesses and particularly handicapped people.

The path meets the old cobbled path to East Town in Butts Lane and continues, via Butts Lane, past the back of the new houses in The Butts and the new bungalows in the lane. Then, after passing Mr Chappell's butcher's shop which has now been converted into a dwelling, the path returns to the High Street. There is a smaller path known as Nannypugs, which diverts from the main footpath and meets the High Street opposite Church Farm.

The Smithy

THE LONG'S ARMS

This old inn was once known as the Coach and Horses where passengers en route from Salisbury to Bath could rest. It has been extended by a single storey building housing the bars. Painted on the wall above the door are clasped hands over the word FELLOWSHIP, rather faded now and only revealed when the covering name board is taken down for repainting. Many have found fellowship here and many have found justice, not always to their liking, because this was the place where the Whorwellsdown Magistrates sat before the village hall was built.

Over the windows other signs were painted on the stone, advising of teas and stabling. The inn sign stands on a patch of green, surrounded by whitened stones to warn off careless motorists. From time to time spoilage of this green has been a bone of contention between landlord and parish council. On more than one occasion the council has threatened to remove the green altogether which would have meant the abolition of the attractive Long's Arms sign but the sign remains and amity prevails. For many years it was the tradition for the customers to come out from the Long's Arms on New Year's Eve to sing 'Auld Lang Syne' as they linked arms, dancing round this green!

AN OLD POND

There is an old stone house standing in the garden opposite the Long's Arms. Once it had been two cottages which were renovated to a superior standard by Mr Frank May who had worked for many years on the restoration and new building at Ashton House under the supervision of Sir Harold Brakspear.

Parish Council correspondence of 1930–32 reveals that garden land transferred to the Parish Council from the Long's Estate was sold to Mr May, the owner of the adjoining property. This land lies between the house and garden of The Lodge. With the correspondence is a note in Canon Knubley's handwriting, stating: 'In the Tithe Award Map of 1821 the greater part of this land is marked as a pond.' Many older residents blamed the flooding in the High Street on the fact that this pond had been filled in. It is also said that there had been almshouses in the vicinity, a fact which seemed to have been borne out when some foundations were found when the garden was cultivated.

A note from a WI member in 1955 reported that Mr May's grandfather and a Mr Berrett from Silver Street both lived to be 100 years old. Both wore a top hat and smock coat. Mr Applegate senior was a regular worshipper at church in 1930 and he also wore top hat and a frock coat and carried a silver-topped walking stick.

In the Steeple Ashton and Great Hinton Newsletter of March 1975 a contribution from Mr May's daughter, Mrs Linda Thompson, stated that her grandfather had died at the age of 103! I know of no other inhabitant who lived to that great age. Mr Frank May had a carrier's business until 1915. Its slogan was 'Willing to carry anything'. He owned a brougham, a one-horse closed carriage, and on special occasions he wore a top hat and red jacket.

THE MERCHANT'S HALL

This impressive old building acquired its title after it ceased to be a post office and shop. It had been three houses. The dormer windowed part nearest to the Long's Arms was once a store shed. I have an old undated photograph showing it without the dormer window and there was no inn sign outside the Long's Arms. Neither had the cobbled path been mended with paving slabs south of the Black Barn Farm gates.

The timbered and herring-bone brick building, recently restored, had been divided. The front door belonged to 'The Cottage' and the low canopied window belonged to the Middle Shop. This is where Judge Jefferies is erroneously supposed to have lodged. There are still some people who remember it as Case's Shop – with bakery, of course. Others recall Mr Bob Watts who had lost a leg – a below knee amputation. He had an artificial leg which he wore when driving his car – he had a hackney carriage licence – and when gardening, but when he was in the shop he used neither artificial limb nor crutches. He would put one hand on the counter and leap over to get supplies from across the shop. A later owner acquired the nickname 'Nooga' because he rejected the local pronunciation of Nugget for the favouite French sweetmeat, Nougat. His successor, Mr Tugwood, gave interviews to the press on the subject of the ghost he had seen. He threw a shoe at it and it disappeared into a cupboard. I believe he said it was a lady in grey, but no-one seems to have seen her since.

Old Merchant's Hall – Middle Shop

The small room to the right of the now closed-up oak door became the Post Office, which was transferred with the business to the 'Top Shop' by the Watchorns in 1970. The shop reverted to being a private house. Miss Marjorie Bartlett removed from the dormered house into a new flat over the garage and her house reverted to the newly-named 'Old Merchant's Hall'. Dr Clarke's renovations of recent years have been so thoroughly well done that the house is now set to stand for another five hundred years.

THE POST OFFICES

Farmer Colbourne of Damerham, near Fordingbridge, on the Hampshire–Wiltshire border, sent his daughter Jane to school – not an everyday occurrence even for farmers in the 'Hungry Forties' of the nineteenth century. Jane did well and eventually obtained a post as Nursery Governess. She met John Bartlett of Steeple Ashton who was a sign-writer and could, therefore, read and write. They were married at Damerham on 10 February 1866. To mark the occasion the bride received a copy of the Authorised Version of the Holy Bible. Her friend, the donor, recorded the occasion in the Bible, which has passed to her great-grand-daughter. A treasure indeed!

They came to live in Steeple Ashton in the house next to The Old Merchant's Hall, now numbered 38 High Street, with its eighteenth-century porch canopy. Here they kept the Post Office with the red letter box, VR, in the wall. Their son William, the carpenter, and his young family lived with them after the death of his wife, the mother of Marjorie. Lucy, daughter of Jane and John was looking forward to training as a teacher, but her father died also and she remained at home to help her mother run the Post Office and bring up William's young family. During the Boer War when letters came from the soldiers to their families, who were unable to read and write, the Bartletts were called upon to read these precious missives.

When the family moved in later years to the stone cottage on the other side of the Hall the Post Office was transferred with them and there was another hole in another wall to receive the red letter-box. Was this when the dormer window was added, I wonder?

Miss Lucy played the organ at West Ashton Church for many years. She walked, each week, to choir practice and Sunday Services. She stayed for Sunday lunch with friends and her brother William, sometimes accompanied by her nieces and great-nieces, went to meet her after Evensong. When the walking got to be too much for her in her latter years she went by taxi.

Schoolmaster, Mr William Cray, used to visit Mr William Bartlett to play chess in the evenings. One evening he expressed his concern about the school. The cleaner and caretaker had fallen ill and he did not known what to do. Mr Bartlett volunteered his daughter Marjorie as temporary help. In 1977 Marjorie received a Medal, sent by the Queen, for her many years of good service to the school. Her temporary job had been very permanent!

She had a dog named Jack – very good at catching rabbits, so it seemed. When Mr George (Shoppy) Burbidge rode out from Trowbridge on his motor-cycle, with laden side-car, to sell his 'custard' ice-creams, around 1930, he often brought rabbits to sell as well. One day he left his motor-cycle combination outside the Longs' Arms while he went in for some liquid refreshment. Miss Bartlett was delighted when Jack brought in a rabbit and of course she praised him lavishly. She was somewhat surprised when he brought in another and absolutely mystified when he re-appeared with a third one. This time she followed him and soon discovered the source of his finds!

As children we were delighted when 'Shoppy' appeared with his ice-creams. Children of today are tempted by the ice-cream man. Now he comes in a mobile shop, complete with musical chimes. Some mothers are known to wax quite musical themselves when the sound of the chimes is heard in the distance. Mother starts to sing a rousing song to drown the approaching music and so prevent the youngsters from wanting ice-creams at unsuitable times. Our penny cornets seem to cost the earth at fifty pence a time these days. Mr Burbidge used to ring a hand bell, like the old school bell, in the manner of the Muffin Man of London Town. The Wall's Ice-Cream man rode a tricycle, with a large cold box on the front bearing the legend, 'Stop me and buy one'. If we had a penny we were pleased to stop him to buy a 'Snofruit', a triangular-shaped lolly, which was most refreshing.

Eighteenth-century porch

After Miss Lucy's day the Post Office continued to be managed for several years by her niece and great-niece, until about 1950 when it was transferred to the Middle Shop, owned then by the Tugwood family. The letter-box transferred again, almost to its original spot. There it remained until 1970 when it transferred again to its present place at the Bennetts' Top Shop, now The Post Office Stores.

The first Post Office mentioned was at No. 38. This cottage and its neighbour both have the eighteenth-century porch canopies and both were occupied for many years by staff from Ashton House. The gardener-handyman of my young days was ex-sailor Mr West, who managed the central-heating boilers situated in the neighbouring cottage, next to Ashton House. Prior to the building of the Village Hall, and presumably the installation of the central-heating, this small property was known and used as 'The Reading Rooms'. Mr Bosanquet was the owner and it was he who provided the money, some as a gift and some as a loan, for the new Village Hall in 1899. The 'Reading Room' was transferred to the new club or committee room, where men would go to read the newspapers of the day.

ASHTON HOUSE

The most important building in the village in the early sixteenth century, apart from the church, was probably Ashton House. This fine Tudor house overlooked the village green where the markets were held and justice was dispensed by the Hundred Court of Whorwellsdown, so we are told. More than once in its long life this old Tudor house has been altered, added to and subtracted from, but the hall and many of the original beams in its walls and roof remain, exposed to view, thanks to the work of Sir Harold Brakspear.

For almost three hundred and fifty years it was the home of the Stileman or Stillman family. It seems reasonable to suppose that Ashton House was one of the two houses granted, with some eighty acres of land and various meadows and pastures, to Anthony Stileman in fee by the Abbess of Romsey. Together with his father, Robert, he was a bailiff of the Manor of Ashton. Robert is recorded as a leaseholder under the Abbess in 1478. It seems to have passed from father to son until 1713, although some of the lands seem to have been sold off, for the rent of 1699 was less than that paid in 1500. The John Stileman who died in 1691 was most probably the churchwarden whose initials IS appear on the new boss in the re-built south aisle after the collapse of the spire in 1670. When this John's son died in 1713 he was survived by his widow, Christian, who lived until 1765.

The initials CS with the date 1724 appear on the lead drain-pipe of the then newly fronted house. The Georgian ashlared front gave a new and then very modern appearance to the venerable Tudor house. A parapet with five, apparently blocked-up, windows actually hides the medieval stone roof. Just beneath this parapet, over the front door, can still be seen the numbered sun sign of the Sun Fire Insurance Company, which denotes that the house was insured against fire – in 1727 – by Christian Styleman, spinster of Steeple Ashton. It was described as her 'New Dwelling House'. At the same time Thomas Styleman, Maltster, insured his household and stock-in-trade at the house of Christian Styleman for £500. Was he perhaps a brother-in-law or nephew, rather than a son, since she insured the house herself? The fact that she was described as a spinster is not important; I think this term applied equally to an unmarried lady or a widow.

The family was well known and respected in Steeple Ashton where they lived from the time of Henry VIII until the reign of Queen Victoria, when Dr Stillman died in 1843 and his sons sold out to Walter Long and emigrated to Australia. There are still members of the Stillman family living in Australia and during the early 1980s some visited this country to seek out their family home and roots in Steeple Ashton.

After Mr Hardinge-Tyler came to the house in the early 1920s many alterations and additions were made, under the supervision of the well-known architect, Sir Harold Brakspear. Old fireplaces and oak beams were uncovered, painstakingly repaired and restored. Part of the bulding was demolished to make way for new kitchen quarters and a new wing was added to the rear of the house. Our WI records reveal that Mrs Hardinge-Tyler was elected to be a Vice-President and remained so from 1924–33, the whole of the time she resided in the village. The gardens were laid out in the Italian style and have been much enjoyed by visitors, particularly those who have attended the numerous fêtes over past years when much money has been raised for the Nursing Association and the Church, in particular.

Rainwater Head, Ashton House

THE MARKET CROSS

When Samuel Hey died in 1828 he bequeathed his large library with some furniture to his successors. When Canon E.P. Knubley was Vicar from 1897 until 1931 this library formed his study in the old part of the vicarage, now the dining room of the 'Old Parsonage'. He was greatly interested in the history of the village and had easy access to all the old records and he told the story of the village in a small book entitled *The Rise and Fall of Steeple Ashton as a Market Town.* From this I have culled most of the following information.

The Market Cross proclaimed the status of the town. The original pillar or staple believed to have dated from the time of William the Conqueror, 1071, was replaced in the reign of Charles II in 1679 by the present pedestal and column. The cube or 'vase' on which the sundials are marked, together with the ball and surmounting cross and crown in wrought iron work was probably added when repairs were done in 1714, possibly to mark the accession of the Hanoverian King George I. The dials were painted white with black figures; the ball was red, white and blue. The later stonework was said to be plainer than the rest. It must have been a colourful sight.

It is not known what repairs were effected in 1782, during the reign of the second King George, but in 1820, to mark the accession of George IV, the steps appear to have been replaced by a deep plinth of very thin ashlar and the broken base of the column was cut away – all for the cost of £15.

To celebrate the Golden Jubilee of Queen Victoria's reign in 1887, Mr C.E. Ponting, FSA directed further repairs. At a cost of £30, the plinth and step of 1820 were removed, the original moulded plinth was restored and one thick and one thinner step of Portland stone were built as indicated in the picture engraved by J. Storer for the Antiquarian and Topographical Cabinet from a drawing by S. Prout (1783–1853) which was published for the proprietors by W. Clarke, New Bond Street & J. Carpenter, Old Bond Street, Decr. 1809. At the same time the sundials were painted and the wrought iron work renewed.

In accordance with ancient custom the Coronation of Her Majesty Queen

Elizabeth II was commemorated by repairs to the Market Cross. The crown, cross and sundials were replaced. The work was done by Ivor Smith with a little help from his father Herbert. My darning 'mushroom' formed the basis of the mould from which the suns or stars were cast. The new crown and suns were gilded. The markings and dates recorded in this history were renewed by Mr Tom Hibbert.

To celebrate Her Majesty's Silver Jubilee in 1977 both the Church Clock and the Market Cross were re-gilded.

THE BLIND HOUSE

Mr Prout's drawing shows the octagonal stone Blind House, sometimes called the Guard House, which was built in 1773 to provide temporary housing for wrong-doers, generally supposed to be those who had over-indulged in the local ale-houses. This small building just over nine feet in diameter and twelve feet high has a stout oak door, into which is set an iron grill. So long as the iron door, about a foot square, behind the grill is open light and air can penetrate the interior. It is reported that prisoners' families and friends provided more liquid refreshment by way of a pipe passed between the bars of the grill! There was not much comfort in this damp and musty cell which had a stone seat over a hole in the drain for sanitary purposes and an iron bar which may have been a seat or the basis for a seat across the corner. It is generally agreed that the last man to be locked up here after being found drunk subsequently died of pneumonia. This story is part of the family history of my friend Joan, a grand-daughter of the arresting police officer Randall of Semington. This would have been about the turn of this century. However, a Miss Mason said she had been told that the Blind House was not much used after 1860. I think, however, my friend's family, who lived in Trowbridge, must have been correct. Mrs Thompson's memoirs in the Newsletter recalled that her grandmother used to take food for the prisoners around 1830, when they were locked in over-night before being taken to Devizes gaol.

The Market Cross and Blind House

JEFFERIS or THE ROYAL OAK or THE LODGE

Behind the Market Cross on Mr Prout's drawing stands the house now known as The Lodge. Once it was called Jefferis and in the mid-nineteenth century it was The Royal Oak kept by Sidney and Sarah Smith. It is a handsome brick building with stone quoins and a stone parapet, with an imposing front door, especially for an inn. This appears to be another older house with a newer Georgian front. It has Deeds dating from the seventeenth century, also some hidden internal beams.

Sidney's father Thomas was born to Catherine, née White, and John Smith of Edington in 1805 and in 1825, married Alice, the daughter of Hannah and William Long. Alice was born in 1800. Her father William, son of Walter Long, was born in 1758, according to the family tree of Heber Booth Smith from Clarkston, Utah, which came to me via Herbert Charles Smith, grandson of Sidney. Heber's father was Sidney's brother Simon. Simon was born in Steeple Ashton in 1833 and went to the United States, arriving in the Salt Lake Valley in 1859 and moving to Clarkston in 1864. He became the first post-master of Clarkston and the second Bishop of the Clarkston Ward of the LDS Church (Church of Latter Day Saints commonly called Mormons) from 1872 to 1876. This information is given by Bishop LaMar C. Berrett in his book *Down Berrett Way* Vol. 1. which gives the history of the Steeple Ashton Berrett family and others from 1604–1978.

We also learn from this that three more of Sidney and Simon's brothers went to America. Charles married Jane Bailey and died en route for Utah in Iowa in December 1849, three months after being baptized into the Mormon faith. He was only nineteen years old. The two youngest brothers, John and William, emigrated to Utah, apparently after being baptized into the Mormon faith here in Steeple Ashton. It was 1873 before John emigrated. Both were married and died aged fifty-four and sixty respectively. Another brother, Thomas, died of exposure when fighting in the Crimean War, 1854–6. He was only about twenty years old and had been baptized into the Mormon faith in 1849.

Sidney himself was born in 1826. He did not become a Mormon in his life-time but was baptized by proxy in Salt Lake Temple, 18 April 1905 and sealed to his parents in the same temple, 21 September 1965!

Sidney and Sarah had ten children, the eldest Sarah Jane helped Sidney to bring up her younger brothers and sisters when Sarah died in 1870, a month after the youngest son Simon Herbert was born. Sarah Jane was only nineteen years old at this time. She later married a widower, Albert Edward Woods

Moore, who had two children. She added six to the family. Her stepson Edward became blacksmith at Keevil and her son Sidney and nephew Herbert Charles succeeded Albert as blacksmiths in Steeple Ashton. Young Sidney's son George opened the 'Dartmoor Garage' at the corner of Hinton Lane and Herbert's son Ivor is now the village blacksmith.

The buildings at the back of the Royal Oak, some of which have been made into a new dwelling, 'The Coach House', were once Sidney's workshops. He was a carpenter, for like most ale-house keepers he needed a trade to supply him with sufficient income. The census of 1861 shows he employed two men and a boy.

There are a number of stories about Sidney and his family. They seem to have been lively and forthright people, who didn't wilt under adversity. John was for many years the Verger at West Ashton Church. Thomas became the blacksmith at South Wraxall and one of his sons also became a blacksmith, the other becoming a policeman serving at Devizes and Chirton. Charlie's daughter married a Devizes butcher and his son was a carpenter. Sarah Jane's youngest sister Mary married Harry Hine. They moved to Gillingham and with their four sons set up business as Hine Bros, starting on contract threshing and later becoming quarry owners supplying sand and gravel to a large area. One of their pits was at Blashford, Ringwood. In 1953 the scholars and teachers at Steeple Ashton School entertained two former old boys; Herbert Smith and his cousin Henry Jack Hine, son of Mary and Harry, who was Mayor of Shaftesbury in that Coronation year.

William James who signed his name with an X at his marriage to Edith Julia Mattock in 1885 acquired the name 'Jinkie' as a very small boy because of his habit of passing from customer to customer in The Royal Oak and asking for a little 'jinkie'. The name stuck and was in turn passed on to his eldest son William who went to farm at Woolmer Green near the then new Welwyn Garden City in Hertfordshire. The second William passed on his nickname to his eldest son.

One famous tale of Sidney, who was also the bandmaster before the Bull family came into prominence, concerns his donkey.

The donkey strayed and was impounded. The constable took it into the pound, which may have been in the vicinity of the Church and the Manor House. The fee for redeeming the animal was one shilling, or in today's currency five new pence. Some of Sidney's cronies had a bright idea and they went to the pound when it was unattended and lifted the donkey over the fence! We hear that the constable was not amused and who can blame him?

Sidney, we hear, was a very generous host and also joined his customers in the gentle art of elbow bending. Consequently, so 'tis said, times became hard for Sidney and he left The Royal Oak – ale-house keeping was not for him. I wonder whether the death of his wife made the life too difficult for him with his young family? At any rate he moved out and we heard no more of The Royal Oak.

It has been known as The Lodge for many years now. When we came to the village the Applegate family were in residence. Captain Jack Applegate was a familiar figure in his fawn bowler hat. He always walked in a very upright manner, like his father, who always wore a silk topper and frock coat and carried a silver knobbed cane. A true Victorian gentleman. The Applegates were wine and spirit merchants, with a bond warehouse in Wicker Hill, Trowbridge. The present Trowbridge Post Office stands on the site of Applegate's Roundstone Hotel, opposite a later innovation, the wine shop, which in recent years has become the Oxfam shop.

Mrs Applegate is well known in theatrical circles, particularly in Bath, but in the war years she was better known as Mrs Wendy Applegate, an officer in the ATS, and later President of the British Legion Women's Section in the area. In her Steeple Ashton days she was a tireless worker organizing concerts and pantomimes in the village and bringing her Bath theatrical friends to add to the fun. People still say, 'Remember when we used to do this or that with Mrs Applegate?' They still have many happy memories of those far-off days of the '20s and '30s.

When the Applegates moved to Semington the entertainment arrangements were largely in the hands of Mr and Mrs Toby Bull. Many a happy evening began with Mr Bull singing 'Tip-toe through the tulips' to start the audience singing with him. He played the trumpet and was also known for his performances as the Dame in Pantomime. Mrs Bull provided piano accompaniment for concerts, dancing classes, pantomimes and 'Jerusalem' at the beginning of all WI meetings. She was a staunch member. She also taught piano to many of the young chilren, for generations.

The Bull family were prominent members of the Steeple Ashton Band for a couple of generations. They recalled a Queen Victoria Jubilee when they performed on the top of the church tower to mark the occasion. The drum was too big to be taken up the steps inside the tower so it had to be hauled up the outside with ropes dropped over the parapet. Ashton men were not easily daunted, they were full of ingenuity.

One of the treats of Saturday evenings in pre-war years was to listen to the band practising in the garden of The Lodge on fine summer evenings. Those who lived in the centre of the village could listen in the comfort of their own chairs by their doors. Folk who lived further away could always visit friends or gather round the Market Cross to enjoy a free musical evening.

THE GREEN

The houses on the Green have witnessed many happenings over the past centuries; they had a grandstand view of the markets and the fairs of bygone days and the skittles games and fayres of present times. They themselves have undergone changes since their early days a couple of hundred or more years ago.

The imposing building with the stone porch, nearest to The Lodge, was first a house and then a chapel and then became a house again. Baptist meetings had been licensed in 1825 and 1828. In 1864 a dwelling house, most likely the one which bears that date, was taken over as a station of the Baptist Chapel at Bratton. A Sunday school was started in 1874. Part of this house was obviously built on and was the Sunday school that I knew of in 1930. I first knew of this when many of my fellow school children were talking of the anticipated pleasures associated with the 'Annie-verse-airy'. This was a new idea to me and it was some time before I understood they were looking forward to an anniversary celebration, a custom shared with the 'Top Chapel' now known as the Methodist church – no longer 'Primitive'. The lucky children who attended these functions seemed to have a double treat. Some even changed their allegiance in the Autumn at the time of Advent and were able to attend the Church of England Sunday School treat which took place just before Christmas. In my early school days here I was appointed 'chief tea taster'. Miss Burnett would get me to try the first cup and if it was sweet enough for me it was alright for everyone!

The chapel was taken over for use as the first aid post at the beginning of the Second World War and used as a casualty clearing station by the ARP (Air Raid Precautions) wardens. The Chapel numbers dwindled and it closed.

Fortunately the casualty clearing station and first aid post were never used for anything more serious than practice sessions. The civil defence committee in charge of war-time Steeple Ashton held their final meeting on 15 November 1944, when it was no longer necessary for the wardens to go round checking on blackout precautions, calling 'Put that light out!' Windows and doors had to be effectively curtained to prevent even a chink of light being visible from outside. Vehicles had to have dimmed and shaded lights. Bicycles had torches like glow worms in front and red rear lights in addition to red reflectors which had hitherto been sufficient. Mr Ashby no longer needed to store the emergency rations; the fire brigade, decontamination squads, stirrup pump and ladder parties, labour gangs and the messenger service manned by children under eighteen, were all stood down. The mortuary was no longer required. The food officer, Mr G.O. Herbert of Ashton House, and Mrs Tilton of The Strand, billeting officer and in charge of emergency feeding, could now retire, thankful that their services had not been needed in this pleasant place.

In 1947 the chapel was sold and re-converted to a private dwelling house, with its view of the Market Cross, Blind House and Ashton House, and of course The Green where children play as they always have on the grass and steps of the Market Cross, though the notice on The Blind House says, 'NO BALL GAMES'. The traffic alone makes such play very dangerous and house windows would also be at risk. There was a time when a footpath crossed the Green as a way from Dark Lane North to the Top Shop. This has long been grassed over and railings have closed the gap. The old wooden rails became dilapidated and were replaced by iron ones. They have been bent once or twice by incautious passing motorists. They are not nearly so comfortable to swing on and turn head over heels, I'm sure! Just as well because the traffic passes dangerously close to the rails now.

In former days when adjoining properties were owned by one landlord it was often easier to open or close a doorway and transfer a room from one house to another rather than to have the tenants move. The little house next to the chapel house re-acquired its former sitting room after many years. Modern building techniques enabled it to have its coat of rendering removed and its original stone and brickwork revealed and invisibly treated to make it weatherproof. For a short time this was used as an antique shop but it soon reverted to a country cottage in harmony with its neighbours. There are two ancient stone cottages between it and The Old Rose and Crown.

THE OLD ROSE AND CROWN

An unusual and eerie smoky glow over the centre of the village had all the menfolk running down to see where the fire might be – surely there was a powerful searchlight, possibly from the fire service, in the vicinity of the Old Rose and Crown? There were floodlights on that Wednesday evening of 23 January 1985, lighting up the building for the cameras of the film-makers! For the previous couple of days they had converted the interior of the Long's Arms for a film set and now they were using The Old Rose and Crown for the exterior of their film inn.

It certainly looks the part of 'ye olde worlde inn'. It has been an inn for a very long time. It exposes genuine old beams and once it had a sign outside on a piece of green just like that of the Long's Arms of today. When that sign was removed it was replaced by a sign which swung in its wrought iron frame above the door, creaking in the wind. It was de-licensed in 1969 and its sign was taken down and the name changed from Rose and Crown to Old Rose and Crown on a discreet decorated sign beside the front door.

The club room of the Rose and Crown was the meeting place of a Friendly Society, which was formed in 1765 and came to an end through the defalcation of the treasurer – a not unusual story!

The Rules were printed by T. Burrough of Devizes, on a broadsheet which measured twenty-three inches by nineteen inches. It was a copy of a Standard and the heading of it contained a representation of two hands clasped under the motto 'Let brotherly Love Continue'. Below was a beehive – a sign of industry. On the left was a good Samaritan under an oak tree round which was entwined a vine. On the right was Father Time, winged, with an hour-glass and a scythe in his hands. Behind him was a human skeleton with a barbed spear directed towards his heart. On the left of the Standard was this verse:

> 'Arise' says Samuel 'Arise and see,
> The prudent conduct of the humble bee,
> There's time allowed for all things here below,
> A time for Joy, a time for Pain and Woe
> And as mankind was born to Grief and Care,
> In Summer thou for Winter storms prepare.'

On the right side was the following verse:

> 'See how the oak supports the feeble vine,
> How close their branches are entwined,
> How Heaven born Charity doth sustain
> And brings a Cordial to relieve his Pains.
> How winged Time as swift as lightning flies.
> Behind him – Death – then learn, be timely wise.'

Rules and Orders to be observed and kept by a Friendly Society instituted at the Rose and Crown Inn, Steeple Ashton, on the 28th day of September 1765. Whereas several Tradesmen, of sundry callings, who have set their hands, have met together in order to provide for the support of each other in Times of Adversity:

We, Members of this Society, inhabiting in or near the Parish of Steeple Ashton aforesaid, taking into consideration the many casualties incident to human nature, and being unwilling to become burthensome to the Parish wherein we live, have thought fit and convenient to join together in an orderly, loving, peaceable and brotherly manner, to provide for the comfortable relief of each other, in times of sickness and lameness, after the method following:

IMPRIMIS

then follow XXV rules. The age limit for admission was 45 years, if in doubt the Register – presumably Baptismal – was to be produced. The two-hourly meetings were to be held once in every six weeks. Each member should contribute one shilling to be laid in stock for the good of the fraternity and twopence to be spent in company and the beer to be delivered into the room at the appointed time. A pension of three shillings a week was payable at the age of sixty if the person had been a member for twenty years. Absence on two consecutive meetings without sending his part meant that his money should remain in stock and he should be excluded. Rule VI: 'That there shall be a Feast held every year on Whit Monday and every member shall pay his dues towards the same, viz: sixpence the second meeting before the Feast and one shilling the first meeting before the Feast or in failure to forfeit sixpence. And every member shall attend Divine Service on such Feast Day and walk with the Clerk and Stewards in a decent manner, each person having a wand in his hand and ribband in his hat, or forfeit two shillings and sixpence for each offence, viz. five shillings for the whole.'

The surplus food from the Feast was used to provide next day's breakfast 'for those whom it may please to come' – before nine o'clock.

The funds provided for a death grant – the clerk to manage the funeral and any surplus money due to him to be given to his wife or other appointee. Members were invited by the stewards to attend funerals, absentees paid a forfeit of one shilling. Death by smallpox exempted these arrangements.

This Friendly Society was not the only one to hold its meetings in the club room. For many years there was a Slate Club into which members paid subscriptions, drew sickness benefit and held an annual share-out at Christmas, but I think it was unfortunate to fall ill in December as sickness benefit could not be paid out when the books were closed for the reckoning for the share-out. Nowadays, I understand the present owners are enthusiastic members of a Scottish Dancing Society who avail themselves of the club room spaciousness.

In the early days of the British Legion, before it became Royal, meetings were held in the public houses of the various villages where members lived. Smoking concerts were regularly held at the Rose and Crown, Steeple Ashton. Here men met and after business they would enjoy their pipes and pints, telling jokes, being entertained and joining in the singing of their favourite songs – some, they said, were not suitable for ladies' ears!

For fifty years Mr and Mrs Arthur Brown were the licencees. He carried on his business of painter and decorator during the day while she kept house and inn. His hobby was breeding black cocker spaniels in the 1930s.

Mrs Brown told me that in the early days, around 1900, if she was not up by six o'clock the carters would be knocking on the door wanting their ale for breakfast. Tea and coffee were expensive and ale was the usual beverage at that time. (My grandmother was offered ale for breakfast when she was a student at the Diocesan Training College, Lincoln a hundred years ago in the 1880s!)

The farm workers at harvest time had a special brew of weaker beer in four gallon jars or cider in two or three gallon jars slung behind the wagons that went to the hay or harvest fields. This practice was common until well into the twentieth century.

For Mrs Brown ten o'clock at night was a welcome closing time. Like most village housewives she would walk to Trowbridge for her shopping, which was not available or perhaps so cheap in the village. She returned with a heavy shopping bag in each hand along Green Lane, which for many years formed part of the main route for coaches from Salisbury to Bath.

One of the things Mrs Brown is remembered for is the caramels which the boys enjoyed. They bought them eight for a penny and went off down Fishponds or Sandpits Lane to eat them!

During the Great War it was recognized that special control of liquor traffic was necessary to encourage national economy and efficiency. The Prime Minister, Mr Lloyd George, even suggested Prohibition but eventually a compromise was reached and whisky went up in price from three and sixpence to twelve shillings and sixpence a bottle and the strength of war-time beer was greatly reduced. Opening hours were restricted and Mrs Brown was no longer required to serve ale at six in the morning. 'Hard work never killed anyone', she would say and she remained sprightly and active into her eighties.

Old timers have said that there used to be a blacksmith's shop on the corner of Church Street and High Street apparently in the garden or even in the place where the neighbouring cottage is now. Do the filled-in gaps in the stone and brick of the house in Church Street indicate that it was once actually joined on to that building? Opinions differ, but I have seen a photograph – there should be a copy in the WI Scrapbook – of an old, slightly tumbledown thatched building with a thatched open porch, possibly the shop, complete with a horse, but I have never met anyone who could actually remember its presence, but 'everybody knows it was there'.

TOP SHOP now THE POST OFFICE STORES

Facing the Rose and Crown is the present Post Office, which has been in the Top Shop since 1970. Beside the main shop is the drapery department and the dwelling house is a shy little Georgian building rather overshadowed by the wall of Ashton House. The Georgian house retains all its original features and no-one can remember it having been altered.

The shop inside has been modernized and is partly self-service for those who wish to choose without assistance but help is always readily available. When I first knew it Mr Lane kept the grocery side and Mrs Lane the drapery side. He was famous for his fine cooked ham and rich fruit cakes and wonderful icing skills. He came from a family of bakers at Bitterne, Southampton and was an excellent baker. The counter then was made of best mahogany, with glass-topped biscuit tins displayed at an angle in front, with another mahogany fitment for more tins, and a glass cupboard displaying mouth-watering chocolates. As children we used to go from shop to shop deciding how to spend our Saturday penny. A farthing would buy a sherbert dab or a licorice bootlace, some sweets could be had for a penny an ounce and bluebird toffees were twopence a quarter-pound! The chocolates were not affordable!

Soap, soda, blue bags, bleaches, disinfectants, candles, washing lines, scrubbing brushes, paraffin and Mansion polish, blackleading, scrubbing

The 'Top Shop' and Post Office

brushes, mops and brooms were all to be had in the village shops. Most of them are stocked today, together with detergents, garden supplies and frozen foods. The ice-cream – a kind of frozen custard – was home-made by Mr Lane. There were no electric deep-freezers or even refrigerators in those shops. The ice-cream tub stood in a bigger container surrounded by salted ice. The aprons and silk stockings, sold by Mrs Lane and Mrs Ashby gave place to nylon tights, toys and gifts.

Mr Mason the plumber lived next door. He was said to be the only man who knew where all the water pipes were in the village. He was instrumental in installing piped water into many homes when it first came to the village in 1913. He watched over the pumping station in Hinton Lane, its windows now blocked up, near to the new large poultry houses. He checked the reservoir near Newleaze and mended leaks in the old lead pipes which burst in icy weather and cold houses, before pipes were lagged as a matter of course. Old Tommy could tell many a good tale in his Scot's accent.

Sometimes when I pass the neighbouring house I hear Mr Victor Berrett playing his piano and I think of the days when he and his brother were members of a local dance band that played regularly for the dances in the village hall, or sometimes after church fêtes in the vicarage garden. The old fashioned dances were much more dignified than the strange hops of today. Besides the waltzes and quick-steps there were many lively polkas. The girls used to wear long dresses for these occasions, some lucky ones wore 'gowns'. The boys wore their best suits and their hair well Brylcreemed. 'Twas no wonder there were always chairbacks, the old word was antimacassars, on the best furniture!

Mistletoe Cottage, with its old bricks and timber frame is another house recently restored which once was two homes. The Burbidge family lived here, Mrs Burbidge being a very hard-working lady who was always ready to help, like many of her neighbours and contemporaries, with charitable functions. She was one of the early stalwarts of the Women's Branch of the British Legion. Her husband Ted was in charge of the engine at the Estate yard and blew the whistle for time. Their large family are all long lived and in the Radio Bristol Compass programme of June 1986, son Bill said: 'I come from a family of eleven and all of us are alive today, totalling in age 800 years. Not a bad record!'

The little rank next door is also very old. Here again there were once three cottages. In the centre, with the large outside chimney, was a little, one up-one down, cottage. At another time the bedroom was part of the neighbour's house and the downstairs was the Snob's or Cobbler's shop, long since redundant. These houses have recently undergone a little restoration and alteration.

The occupant of the house opposite, now called Goodards – then The Laurels was one of the public-spirited men who came to the rescue by

Mistletoe Cottage

providing a lamp at his gate to illuminate the road. The question of street lighting was regularly raised at meetings of the Parish Council after it was first elected from the parish meeting of December 1894.

In 1899 it was decided that necessities such as water and drainage were to be put before the luxuries of street lighting! In 1906: 'This Meeting of Steeple Ashton begs to tender its hearty appreciation and thanks to Messrs E. Tucker, H.E. Tucker and W. Chester for their generosity and welfare for the public good shown by them in providing and maintaining lamps for lighting portions of the village during the winter months.' So Mr E. Tucker of The Laurels was thanked. In 1907 Mr Cary offered to place and maintain lamps outside his sister's house and by the churchyard wall at the top of Church Farm garden. Street lighting was a subject raised at many more parish meetings and at last, in 1950, it was reported that the street lighting since the previous September had proved to be a great improvement!

From this point to the boundary at Bleet on the Melksham road, a mile away, there remain but four farms where once there were nine. Most of them had milking cows in 1939. The first farm to go was Tyler's Farm on the corner of Church Street. When old Mr Woodman died his house was sold but his fields were left to the Church and let to another farmer for cattle grazing. Others that became just private houses after the last war were Thorn Farm, the eighteenth-

Church Farm

century brick house opposite Goodards, and its neighbour on the other side of Butts Lane and opposite Tyler's, Ball's Farm. This was an even older stone house with stone roof, the buildings of which supported the old AA sign, giving the mileage to Trowbridge 5 and to London 96, and where we had seen 'VOTE FOR LONG' when first we came to Steeple Ashton. In its former orchard and paddock are the new houses, executive style, in The Butts.

Church Farm on the opposite side of the Church Street to Tyler's is still very much a farm. The house is very old, the side reveals the brick and beams of Tudor times but the jettied front is no more; it was built under and roughcast over to weatherproof the front. It has an outside stone chimney and a recently repaired old stone tiled roof. It is separated from its very modern neighbours by its tall black wooden barn, now a garage rather than a hay barn.

Its neighbours are, like the ones in The Butts, of modern red brick and large and imposing. In front of them there are flowering trees in the grass. The trees were planted in memory of Mr E. Leventon, JP, a former parish council chairman, farmer and magistrate, a kind and highly respected gentleman. The ground where they were planted was once the pond known as Rail Pond. In 1933 the white rails were removed, although the pond had been filled in during 1922 as its condition had been blamed for the diphtheria which caused the death of Irene Matthews of Bartlett's Farm, opposite. This house again is old brick with stone quoins and had a large dairy at the rear. The Irene Matthews of the next generation is now Mrs Jefferies who now lives at Bartlett's Farm. The family no longer keep cows, the menfolk contract for agricultural work and are well thought of because of the care they take in leaving young trees in the hedges they cut, so that the elms which succombed to the Dutch Elm disease will, hopefully, be replaced.

On Tuesday, 26 June 1973, I made a note in my diary to say that my grandson, Matthew, aged almost two years had been looking through the window of his Church Street home when he cried out to tell his mother 'that tried to hurt my head'. 'That' was the lightning which struck the big black barn and caused it to burn to the ground, without damaging the small and very ancient cottage in front of it, which boasted a pear tree on its end wall for

Black Barn Farmhouse

many, many years. Now there is another new housing estate on the site, called Bartlett's Mead and the little cottage and farmhouse are surrounded. The little cottage's other neighbour is a square, cheerful-looking small house with a coat of pebble-dash over its old brick, and its once thatched roof is tiled.

Although the lightning strike did not set fire to any other properties it did cause the electricity meter to be thrown from the wall of the tall brick house opposite the Methodist Church. The occupant, Mr Bolt, an elderly ex-Marine, was thrown to the floor across the kitchen but he recovered and lived a further four years. He made a fine speech of thanks to his neighbours and good friends of Steeple Ashton when he opened the church fête at Ashton House in the Queen's Silver Jubilee year, 1977. The people were all very sad when he died a mere three weeks later at the ripe old age of ninety-two.

THE METHODIST CHURCH

There is a wonderful story told of the Methodist Church which was built in 1854. There was a big mortgage on the building. The mortgagee called in the money which the church members were unable to pay and the Church was put up for auction at Devizes. The members held a united prayer meeting asking that it would not be sold. One of the Elders, Mr Elijah Bull, attended the auction to watch the sale. Not a single bid was received and the property was not sold. The members considered this a direct answer to their prayers and set to work to pay off the mortgage. This they did and were able to pay for re-seating and re-decoration in 1914.

The Church was licenced for weddings in 1904 and Mr and Mrs Frank May were married there. They lived opposite the Long's Arms for many years. Methodist Church weddings are rare events.

Faithful members have presented gifts, a clock, an oak chair, brass flower vases and money. Mr May made the altar table. A new organ was given in memory of Mrs Olive Smith who had played the old one for sixty-six years. Her father, Mr John March, had been a steward and trustee. There are memorial tablets to some of the elders and local preachers.

The circuit ministers and local preachers take the services. The present minister is a lady, the Revd Edmee Hurst, who lives in Trowbridge. In this present era Methodists and Church of England congregations, once unfriendly rivals, meet and worship together in fellowship and friendship.

The Methodist Church and Cottages

ST MARY'S

A special meeting was called in December 1918 to consider the building of workmen's dwellings. The decision was deferred because it was thought that costs would be too high; the rents would be five shillings a week, about one sixth of a man's wages, and it was possible there would be a deficit to be made good by the parish. In 1919 it was decided to ask the Rural District Council to build the houses. They appointed an architect, Mr G. Stanley. Building was slow because of the shortage of bricks in 1920, houses 'fit for heroes to live in' were being built all over the country.

They were completed and have provided council housing ever since until one or two were bought by tenants. The remainder have recently been renovated and modernized. Originally the back doors were approached from 'The Drive', a service track gated off from the High Street.

The front doors are on the sunny side, facing down the long gardens. During the past ten years or so 'The Drive' has been widened and made into a good road to accommodate further housing on the fields of the former Rose Farm. The West Wilts District Council has built garages, bungalows for the elderly and family houses on this site.

The field at the end was sold to the Wiltshire County Council for a new school in the 1970s. Circumstances and numbers changed and the school building plan was shelved, but the playing field is used and is in the care of the Parish Council. There is a children's playground and facilities for the Football Club. The cheering can be heard all over the village when home matches take place on Saturday afternoons. The field was the venue for the barbecue held to celebrate the wedding of the Prince and Princess of Wales.

The extended one of the pair of semi-detached houses at the corner of St Mary's and the High Street was a county police house until 1934 or thereabouts. Rose Farm encircled these.

ROSE FARM

Standing in its large, well tended, garden on the corner of High Street and Sandpits Lane was the small thatched and timbered cottage with its base of stone. At one time the pretty garden was so overgrown that the cottage was almost hidden from view. In his collection of slides Mr Bryan Berrett has a picture showing just that. Many remember it before it was pulled down to make way for new bungalows, well built, substantial and convenient, not picturesque!

Mr March, a trustee of the Methodist Church, farmed the land for most of his life, helped in his latter years by his son 'Young John'. Old Jack, as he was known, grew vegetables in his large garden, as well as keeping a herd of milking cows, selling some of the milk at the back door, as was the custom. Like his brother-in-law, Mr Turner of Coach Barton, he took his produce to Trowbridge on a flat-bed pony cart. When he died in 1945 that same pony and cart carried him in his coffin to his last service at the Methodist Church en route for burial in the churchyard of St Mary's Church.

In the farm-yard was a well, now safely sealed beneath the floor of the utility room in the bungalow which replaced the cottage farmhouse. Donkeys were used as much as ponies before 1914 and the Rose Farm donkey fell down the well. Daughter Olive, who was organist at the Methodist Church from the age of thirteen until she died, some sixty-six years later, in 1983, grabbed the donkey's rope and screamed until help arrived to pull the donkey safely out. Her mother Mrs March was one of Steeple Ashton's nonagenarians.

As well as the council properties there are three more bungalows on this former farm land, entered from Sandpits Lane, known for many years as Fishponds, because it led to the lake of Rood Ashton House, made to provide employment in the hungry years when harvests were poor between 1840 and 1850. The lake, properly known as Stourton Water, was made from three smaller lakes. An old lane was closed off, farm buildings demolished and trees planted to improve the vista from Rood Ashton House.

SANDPITS LANE – NEW HOUSING

Among the new houses on the opposite side of the lane and the bungalows up Gullivers Lane is a much older red brick house. This was once the home of another Burbidge family. 'Old Bill' Burbidge was a builder who employed many men to work on council housing projects – they built the first ones at Edington about 1921 – between the wars. He was a staunch member of the church choir. His daughter Dolly used to give my elder daughter a ride on her bicycle when delivering newspapers in Dark Lane in 1945 and 6. After her death the property was sold, the workshops and stores pulled down to make way for the Gullivers Lane development around 1963.

The field that had been Farmer Joby Woodman's gift to the Church was sold. For a time it was let for cow pasture and eventually it was sold for housing development. In 1970 the present Holmeleaze estate was built and houses and bungalows face a pleasant roadway with unfenced gardens. It was about this time too that the new houses were built in the former paddock and orchard of Ball's Farm, now named The Butts.

NEWLEAZE

Some time after 'Dartmoor' Garage was built on the corner of Hinton Lane the Rural District Council built two pairs of smaller council houses opposite, at right angles to the main road. As at St Mary's there was no road in front or behind them; access was along a wide footpath. Cars were still scarce before 1939 and very few were owned by the tenants of council houses.

The men who returned from War service, soldiers and civilians alike, were in urgent need of houses and the remainder of Newleaze was soon planned. In 1947 Mr A.A. Bull, a Chapel Elder and Chairman of the Steeple Ashton Parish Council, laid the first brick for the first of fourteen new houses and in 1953, Coronation year, a further twenty-two were begun. Since 1980 many tenants have become owner-occupiers.

The decline in the demand for allotment gardens to rent has led to an increasing number of new houses on the stretch of the main road opposite the Newleaze housing estate. The new Police House, nearest to Loppinger Farm, was first built about 1934 or 5. It is now many years since a police officer lived here. The house has been sold more than once and has trebled in size. Next door is a bungalow, built pre-war by Mr Phillips for his own use; this too has changed hands and grown into a house! The fine house next door which once had a large orchard – hence its newer neighbour's name, was the third house on this side before 1939. The remaining houses are much more modern.

The Steeple Ashton nameplate is a good half-mile from the old AA sign on Ball's Farm wall. Over the hedge are the sheep of Loppinger Farm, grazing as did their many predecessors for as long as I can remember. The tall Poplar trees which stood sentinel at the gateway have sadly gone and the gate itself has been replaced by a cattle grid on the long lane which leads to the ancient farmhouse.

TOP OF THE COMMON

The new buildings here have had about thirty or forty years in which to blend with the older cottages, though some of these have been more recently renovated. The new shed is a replacement for a much older one of uncertain age which threatened to fall into the road.

Ashton Hill Farm has its farmhouse on the north side of the road and some of its barns on the corner of Mudmead Lane on the opposite side of this tricky bending road. This farm is worked in conjunction with Loppinger Farm, both belonging to members of the Sims Family, who have lived at Loppinger for as long as anyone can recall.

As early as 1921 the residents at the Common asked for boards to be erected to warn motorists of the danger of going too fast at Mudmead Lane. This lane leads via Lyneham Way to Sandpits Lane beside the lake. A second board was requested for the bottom of the hill, where the road bends left towards Trowbridge. In the days before there were HALT or more lately STOP signs, this was a very tricky junction. In response to the Parish Council's request the Rural District Council advised: 'Write to the RAC direct.' There were no signs. Fortunately there have so far been no fatal accidents at these spots, but plenty of near misses! In times past Mr Geoffrey Bennett and his son John lived higher up the hill and both worked for the County Council on the roads. As long as they lived there the road was well gritted early on frosty mornings, but after they moved away the road was no longer gritted and one or two motorists had hair-raising experiences because of ice on the road at the Mudmead Lane corner. Gladly they survived to tell their tales!

THE COMMON

The heavy lorries have widened the roadway, once known as Common Lane. What was once a pleasant walk down the hill has now become a terrifying

experience, not to be undertaken lightly and not pleasant for cyclists. It was in 1927 when a request was made for the erection of a signpost at the bottom of the hill where the road turns left for Trowbridge, near the telephone kiosk. The villagers complained in 1933 that there was no light in the kiosk near the Long's Arms, but the people of the Common had no kiosk for many more years. Speed limits were posted for the village in 1936, but the Common was and still is excluded from this 30 mph limit. They do now have signs indicating Ashton Common, which pleased the residents and prevented delivery lorries making unnecessary journeys to the village and getting lost.

One of the farms which disappeared completely after the 1939–45 war was the one on the right-hand side of the road going towards Melksham. This was a quaint little thatched cottage of great antiquity, set well back from the road, its nearest neighbours a row of tiny cottages which were separated from their other neighbours by the brook which forms the boundary with Hinton at Bleet.

The telephone exchange for the Keevil area faces these and has both a new bungalow and a new house between it and another row of older cottages on the Melksham side of the Trowbridge road junction. There are old and new houses and bungalows on the Trowbridge road. One old cottage, set well back from the road, was once a weaver's cottage. It still retains the original loom hooks in one of its old beams. For many years it was the home of the blind organist, Mr Henry Brown, and his sister, Miss Bessie. She was a great help to him. In their later years they walked to the church services, twice on Sundays and to the Friday night choir practices in all weathers. He played the organ and she helped him in his choir master duties.

They were not young when I first knew them and I have been surprised to learn of their earlier activities, which have been remembered with affectionate admiration. They had a double bicycle with wide handle-bars so that they sat pedalling side by side and she was able to steer while he just rested his hands on the handlebars. Apparently they travelled some distances like this, chatting away between the hedgerows.

In his younger days when traffic was not so dangerous his dog Rover accompanied him when he walked alone to the village shops or to Church.

Another of his accomplishments was to estimate correctly the weight of a pig. He would lift it up in his arms and announce his opinion of the weight, which was then checked and found to be accurate.

He was kind too. When we were planning our war-time wedding we were told that Mr Brown would like to play the organ for us and there would be no charge. Whether this was because of his friendship with our two families, or because the menfolk had all been members of the choir we were never told. Perhaps it was his contribution to the welfare of a serving soldier. Certainly, the Vicar, the Revd O.R. Yerburgh, made no charge for the wedding of any serviceman. He was Chaplain to the RAF who served at Keevil. He was especially kind to us on our wedding day. He invited us to use the infants' room at school for our wedding reception on that Saturday after Easter in 1942. A jolly crowd of well-wishers came to share our day, first at church and then in the daffodil decorated schoolroom. A unique occasion!

ASHTON COMMON

There is a little lane with cottages of stone on either side leading up to the former Woodbine Farm. I could never understand why the right-hand cottage should have its back to the pair on the left, unless it was that it had to keep an eye on its other neighbour on the main road when it was the Bath Arms. A former landlord of the Bath Arms, Mr 'Nippy' Griffin, swapped places with small farmer Mr Smith, of Brook Farm. Mr Griffin went to live on the farm bounding the brook called Paxcroft which forms the boundary with Hilperton. One icy day in 1939 I was riding home from Trowbridge in the car with my father when we saw Mrs Smith at the top of the hill by Hilperton Grange struggling to take two large cans of water to her home at the bottom of the hill. She was very grateful to accept a lift as she had fallen more than once on that slippery hill and rarely reached home with her full complement of water. All the roads were very slippery, pipes had burst and she had to go to Hilperton for water as she had no neighbours then. Things had improved before the property transfer. There are neighbours now but they are mostly Hilperton orientated although still in the parish of Steeple Ashton.

The Smith family settled into the Bath Arms for a time but trade was low and eventually they moved away and there was no more Bath Arms.

When we cycled to school we used to ride along with Mr 'Bruin' Wareham of Woodbine Farm as he took his cows along the road to pasture. We admired the gentle way he trained them to walk in file, when with a 'whup there' and a thwack on the rump they moved aside to let the traffic through. We were never afraid to cycle past these mild creatures.

There are quite a few chestnut trees along this end of the Common, very good for conkers! The most striking, when seen from the direction of Trowbridge, are the ones outside New House Farm, where they have the last milking herd of the village. The last farmhouse on the left before the crossroads, Malthouse, ceased to be a farm when Mr Gerrish died.

BULLEN HILL

Between these last two farms is a rather bumpy lane leading to two farmsteads. The stone one on the left, which lost its stone barn annexe in a 1986–7 gale, is the home of the Wareham family who were notable for milking their cows in the fields in the summer time, sitting on the little three-legged milking stools.

They made quite a pretty picture returning home in a pony trap with cans of milk and smiling children.

The two most regular visitors to almost all the homes in the village are the Smith brothers, Godfrey and Michael, who deliver the milk, eggs, butter, cream, soft drinks – fresh orange juice and fizzy lemonade – calling every day in the year, including Christmas Day. On the very rare occasions when they take a day off in pursuit of moths and butterflies, about which they are very knowledgeable, they make an evening delivery as well as a morning delivery so that they can take the day off without depriving their customers of fresh milk. They are very willing to share their knowledge on gardening problems and on any aspect of nature, birds, plants and animals; they know where the rarer birds and the deer are to be found. Originally they kept a dairy herd in the right-hand Bullen Hill farm, but the milk round grew and Godfrey's daughters got married, so the milking herd was exchanged for young stock and they obtain our daily pintas from Unigate.

These happy young men are full of fun and knowledge, keen ornithologists and lepidopterists, true countrymen. They take messages in emergencies, deliver notices on items of local interest and have been known to save customers' lives, by calling for medical help when finding a customer sick or collapsed. We cannot speak too highly of our milkmen. They give excellent service. They are grandsons of the late Mr Jack March of Rose Farm and told me, among other things, the story of their mother and the donkey in the well and said Grandpy March had a tame Jackdaw which would sit on the light at the Methodist Chapel waiting to accompany him home!

The farms at Bullen Hill once formed part of a very old settlement which lay between Mudmead Lane and the present Ashton Common road to Trowbridge. A little towards Trowbridge, lying off the main A350/361 between West Ashton and Yarnbrook, is a new farmhouse and a modernized and much enlarged former Keepers Cottage. Although surrounded on three sides by fields these dwellings are not nearly so remote as they used to be, though they must find the traffic on the main 'Turnpike Road' rather trying for there is a constant roar which can be heard for quite a distance along the Common. Of course they now have telephones which the former inhabitants of Keepers Cottage would not have had, or maybe even dreamed of.

Crossways Farm is right beside the crossroads, although alterations to the shape of the crossroads have given them more breathing space and eliminated the prospect of repetition of the accidents of the 1930s when cars were known to somersault into the front garden!

From Crossways Farm the road to Trowbridge takes a sharp bend away from Green Lane, the former Salisbury to Bath Coach road. At either end are homesteads unconnected by a hard road. There is a track, negotiable on foot when the brambles and mud do not hinder. At the end of this track is Green Lane Farm, Trowbridge Rugby Club and the many houses of the post-war Green Lane Estate which forms part of the Parish of Steeple Ashton, sending one more councillor to the Parish Council than the village ward does. There are plans afoot to extend the housing of the Parish across the West Ashton Road to the boundary, the River Biss by Blackball hatches. The existing Green Lane Ward has the Paxcroft Brook for one boundary and has part of the medieval Biss Wood alongside the houses where deer are to be found, which can be seen grazing at dusk in the adjoining fields.

Rural nocturne

What was it like in the Old Days Grandma?

The walkabout is done but there are still many untold and interesting tales. The style and tempo of life in Steeple Ashton, as elsewhere, has changed, perhaps more in the last one hundred and fifty years than in any preceding centuries.

In the present Baptismal Register in St Mary's Church five generations of the Smith family are registered from 1857 when John, later West Ashton's Verger was baptized, 1858 when Grandfather William James appeared until 1972 when young Christopher Brett, the youngest member of the present family, was baptized. Herbert Charles Smith, Bert the Blacksmith knew them all, William James was his father and Christopher his great-grandson, five generations of Steeple Ashton. Reminiscences from Bert's eighty-four years will serve to illustrate the changing scenes of village life.

Bert was born in 1892 when 'Shanks' pony' was the normal form of transport and the petrol engine was being sought after. He died in 1976, seven years after the first man walked on the moon! He saw the first motor car driven into Steeple Ashton when he was a very young man still at school, which he left in 1904. He owned one of the first motor-cycles in the village in 1925 and at the same time he had his Cat's Whisker wireless set. The later sets needed accumulators filled with acid and distilled water to provide electricity to operate them. These were used until the end of the 1939–45 war. The old wireless sets had lots of wire! The one in the school in the late 1920s had an aerial stretching the length of the playground and was attached to a pole or 'mast' almost thirty feet high. The birds enjoyed it. The swallows, swifts and martins gathered on the aerial for their annual migration to Africa in August and September.

Bert enjoyed television in his sons' homes. The first television sets appeared in the village in the 1950s and enjoyed a boost at the time of the Coronation in 1953. Reception was not always good and TV owners could be seen prowling along looking for people using unsuppressed electrical equipment which interfered with the pictures. It was the mid-1960s when television sets began to be commonplace and Chris Noad was kept busy supplying and repairing sets and collecting the rents, for most of them he rented out.

Like most of his contemporaries Bert went to school when he was three. This custom continued in Ashton until the Second World War. Miss Burnett, the infants' teacher, agreed to take them in as long as they were toilet trained and could ask to leave the room. The little children played with sand and sticks and plasticine, had a nap after dinner and then progressed into the infants' class when they showed more interest in lessons than in play and teacher considered them competent or when they were five years old and it was then a compulsory move.

In 1902 Bert received what he thought was a unique award. He had received a medal in 1901 for six years unbroken attendance and in 1902 he received a silver watch chain, together with a certificate, which we have framed even now, '– for seven years unbroken attendance in the Steeple Ashton National School'. He was very proud of his achievement. He left school when he was twelve, having passed the appropriate school-leaving examination. He went to live in Vine Cottage with his Aunt Jane and was apprenticed to her husband, Albert Edward Woods Moore, the blacksmith. He later became a journeyman with Albert's sons, after Albert died in 1910.

He liked to tell the story of the time when he took over the blacksmith's shop

Ivor, the village blacksmith at work

on his own. He had to report to Rood Ashton for an interview with the Squire which went something like this: 'You were one of my recruits weren't you' – this referred to the recruitment of soldiers in 1914 when Bert was rejected on account of his flat feet. Those same feet had prevented him following another cousin into the Wiltshire Police Force at an earlier date. Bert agreed with the Squire's 'You got snubbed'. 'I want you to take over the blacksmith's shop and to shoe my horses.' 'Very good, Sir', and that was how the agreement was made. When the Estate was sold in 1929–30 Bert bought the blacksmith's shop and his house in Church Street, as he recalled for the *Bristol Evening World's* reporter Bernard Birks in an interview in 1959. In the early days as well as shoeing horses they mended ploughs, gates and any other metal work. Housewives brought pans and kettles for repair and the grindstone was often in use for sharpening knives, scissors, sickles and chisels, in spite of the itinerant knife-grinder who came with his barrow and dog. This man was considered to be surly and bad tempered and his dog was no better – maybe he found it hard to make a living, especially as the more modern-minded young wives had stainless steel knives. He was an old man in a dying trade.

The farm horses had to be shod while the carters were at lunch. The horse would be brought up at twelve o'clock and had to be shod ready for collection on the return to work for one o'clock. For as long as he lived Bert's dinner hour was from more or less one fifteen until two fifteen. Old habits died hard with him! Those horses that could not be shod in the lunch hour had to be done after tea, often after dark, when the horses returned from their day's work. His son Ivor recalls holding a candle so that his father could see where to put in the nails.

Ivor would receive a clip on the ear if the candle was not held both steady and in the right place, for a nail in the wrong place could so easily lame a horse and that was a serious matter. Mr Stuart White had a horse called Duke, reputed to be the biggest horse around here. Duke's shoes were ten inches wide. Mr Billy Cox of Bratton worked for the County Council and his big grey horse that drew the carts of gravel was the last big one to be shod in Steeple Ashton, by Ivor in the 1960s.

The number of horses and ponies dwindled during the war years and Bert was ill and unable to shoe horses after 1948. He tried once or twice on quiet horses but it did his old heart no good. However, he continued to make the shoes until he was 79 years old. Ivor would go out to shoe the horses after he had finished his day's work as an agricultural blacksmith, making elevators, seed drills and the like and assisting with repairs to machinery and bonding wheels at Bratton for R.J. Reeves and Son. His customers would often fetch him after tea and return him home much later when the horses were shod and stabled. Often he would work for most of Saturday and on occasion even on Sunday mornings. But this latter went rather against the grain with him, yet more people had leisure and took to horse riding, especially the children. The Pony Clubs encouraged the youngsters to learn to ride. The Horse of the Year Show and the eventing and show-jumping at the Olympics caused a new fashion. He went to Larkhill School of Artillery to shoe Captain Templar's horse 'M'Lord Connolly' which was entered for the Tokyo Olympics. After twenty years at Bratton 'THE FIRM' closed down and there is now a green and a housing estate where once many men worked at the forges in the blacksmiths' shop.

Ivor carried on the business at Steeple Ashton and having bought a car he continued to visit his customers over a twelve to fifteen mile radius, sometimes accompanied by up to three retired companions who enjoyed the ride and were happy to lend a hand to catch or hold a horse. In the shop they would blow the bellows and hand the tools, all with much joking and leg pulling and great good humour. Happy Days!

It was traditional for old men and the unemployed to gather at the forge to pass the time. During the Depression Years after 1926 there were many such and Bert could always be depended upon for a 'tanner for a packet of fags' – sixpence for cigarettes. Woodbine cigarettes were the cheapest, five for twopence. The more expensive at that time were ten for sixpence – a real luxury.

There were many men who enjoyed the pastime of 'ha'penny nap' – the card game called 'Nap' for a half-penny stake! This wasn't strictly legal, it was classified as gambling and in consequence the village 'Bobby' was anxious to catch them and enforce the law. They had many dodges for evading his vigilance and would stroll down a lane and sit where they could keep watch on all sides – that is unless they got too engrossed in the game. One Sunday evening, so 'tis said, they were enjoying a quiet game when just in time they saw the policeman approaching. Hastily they concealed the evidence and nonchalantly greeted the man in blue. He fixed his eye upon the youngest of the party and remarked that he looked pale, wasn't he very well. Quick as a flash, they said, one member replied that the poor lad was a little out of sorts as he had had some cucumber for tea! There was nothing more to be said and the poor policeman retired to gnash his teeth in private, one supposes.

A trip to Trowbridge Market on a Tuesday was once an essential part of village life and the highlight of the week for schoolchildren on holiday. Bert had a pony and trap and was for many years the link between small farmers, housewives and the Market. On Tuesday mornings he would collect calves, pigs, poultry, eggs and perhaps garden produce for sale in the market. For forty years it was a treat for the village children to accompany him on these occasions, provided that there was sufficient room and not too many calves to take. After handing over the stock to the auctioneers' man they would collect the poultry corn and pig meal from the Co-op Corn Chandler's shop and call in the Co-op cake shop next door for doughnuts and lardy cakes. When this cake shop closed down it was even better for then they went to Mrs Moore's cafe and had lemonade as well before the homeward journey. The first children to enjoy these treats were Ivor and his pals. Their cakes were bought from Drew's Bakery in Hilperton Road opposite the Halve, where there is now a roundabout.

When the trains stopped at Edington Station, before 1950, Bert and pony would take the Governess cart to take passengers to catch the train to London or to meet passengers who needed transport home to Steeple Ashton. He also took his wife on the rare occasions when he went to customers at Housecroft, or to Keevil and Bulkington. His grand-daughters enjoyed these trips when they were able to go too. He used to take his bicycle when called upon to deliver telegrams at sixpence a time and for a while he was an auxiliary postman at Christmas and a temporary postman in the days when letters were brought from Trowbridge and left at the local post office for distribution and not delivered, as they are today, by the postman in his van from Trowbridge.

During the last war he was one of the ARP (Air Raid Precautions) wardens, trained in first aid and a member of Steeple Ashton's Volunteer Fire Brigade, like many more of his contemporaries. Fortunately in Steeple Ashton their services were not called upon. After the evacuees from London had left and the construction workers for the aerodrome, only the presence of servicemen and the noise of the planes were there to remind local people of the war which caused shortages and rationing.

Bert was a legend in the football club of his youth. He was a tall man, six foot four in his socks, with long arms and large hands and it was said that he filled the goal mouth and few goals could be scored against him. The Steeple Ashton Football Club has had a good name ever since those Edwardian days when he played in goal and it is still flourishing.

In 1922 there was a sports club with a pavilion in Hinton Lane near to the old pumping station in the field beside the present poultry unit. There was a cricket club which faded out just before the Second World War. The tennis club continued until 1955 and raised a good deal of money, especially during the war years, by organizing the very popular whist drives. Whist drives are still held in the Village Hall on the first Friday evening of each month. Today's young people go away from the village for most of their sport. Clarendon School has facilities for squash and swimming and the pupils enjoy these and also cross-country running and the normal sports in the curriculum. The Trowbridge Rugby Football Club ground is within the parish boundary, but not in the village. There are sports and swimming facilities in Melksham, Trowbridge, Bradford-on-Avon, Westbury and Bath, all within easy reach. Some go to Chippenham and some to the Oasis Sports Centre at Swindon which has a wave machine in the swimming bath. That might not be a novelty for today's generation but it was unheard of when their parents were young. Parents run 'taxi' services among themselves to help the young people to extend their sporting skills enjoyably. Young people of an earlier generation had to cycle to Westbury or Chippenham for a swim unless they cycled to Farleigh Hungerford on the other side of Trowbridge for a swim in the river. This was cold and only suitable as a summer activity.

At an age when Bert and his fellows were out to work, his great grandsons were at school doing O and A level examinations, enjoying cross-country running and squash or discovering the countryside along the Wiltshire Cycle Path, touring the Isle of Wight on bicycles or walking the hills at the Brecon Beacons or the Ten Tors of Dartmoor in May. I went to see the walkers coming in after the wettest walk in the history of this event; some had walked twenty-five miles, some thirty-five and some forty-five miles. Young people from all walks of life, schools, youth clubs, service cadets, in groups of six. It brought a lump to the throat to see their cheerfulness and the spruceness of the Cadets who marched in looking as if they had turned out for Church Parade and gave no sign that they had endured two wet nights on the Moor and carried kit and bedding on their backs for all those miles. That was an experience not to be missed. The youth of Britain are not all yobbos.

These activities are good sport for the present generation but their grandfathers and great-grandfathers would not have had the leisure time or opportunity to enjoy them. Grandfathers cycled five miles or so to school and then to work. Great-grandfathers walked, sometimes it took them an hour or more to walk the six miles or more before they began their day's work and the same time to return at night. Only the dedicated 'keep fit' fanatic would dream of cycling to Trowbridge to work each day, it is so much quicker by car. We do know of some who drive a car half a mile to the Village Hall to attend keep fit classes!

Once the buses that ran to take people to work and bring them home at night were grossly overloaded, but as more people acquired cars the services declined through lack of support as charges went up and times became inconvenient, the number of passengers went down and so began a vicious circle, until now the buses run rarely and perhaps only with one or two passengers where once they were full to capacity with people standing in the aisle. When the Polish and Hungarian refugees inhabited the Airfield hutments people in the village were left behind and the question of bus services appeared on the agenda of the parish meetings in 1948 and 9. In 1948 the question raised was: 'Could the Polish people have a special bus service? People of the village were being left behind!' Also: 'Could there be a bus stop with shelter at Newleaze?' Dr Haythornthwaite asked that there should be a window in the shelter so that older passengers could see the bus coming without having to venture out in the rain. The shelter was provided, with a window, but it wasn't long before it was vandalized and the window had to be blocked up.

Barn at Manor Farm

The Polish people have been settled in their own homes in and around Trowbridge for the past thirty years. The passengers left standing made alternative arrangements and those who want to travel by bus today have to travel on school cum service buses. The Bus Station in Trowbridge has ceased to be and has become a large car park.

OUR EVACUEES

The Government of the day was concerned for the safety of the children of the cities in the event of war. Accordingly after the Munich crisis of 1938 preparations were made for the evacuation of children from the big cities like London and from other places considered to be in the danger zone if war came – as indeed it did. Steeple Ashton was a 'safe area'. A meeting was held and volunteers undertook many duties. Miss Weston, a veteran of 70+ asked, 'What can the over-seventies do?' She was appointed Billeting Officer, but in the summer of 1939 she was replaced by Mrs Dixon – possibly the task was too formidable for one of that age.

On 3 September 1939, Mr Neville Chamberlain made his famous announcement, heard by millions of listeners to his radio broadcast at 11 o'clock on that fateful Sunday morning '. . . this country is now at war with Germany'. Newspapers in the following days were illustrated with photographs showing London railway stations crowded with tearful children and mothers trying to put on brave faces as they parted from each other. The children had gas-masks in boxes slung over their shoulders and with them were their pathetic bundles of luggage. For the mothers with young babies who were also being evacuated it was not quite so bad, but they all presented a pathetic scene.

Steeple Ashton had made preparations to receive its allotted contingent of schoolchildren who were to be brought by coach from Westbury station after their train journey from London. The willing hostesses and prospective foster-mothers were gathered at the Village Hall ready to serve tea. Nurse Collier was to 'look them over' before they were taken to their temporary war-time homes. The expected time of arrival came and went. Repeated enquiries were made and finally it was discovered that 'our' evacuees had been despatched to Westbury on Trym, Bristol, and a coach load of mothers and babies who were expected there were stranded at Westbury railway station, Wiltshire. This was the first day that the 'black-out' regulations came into force, when no lights were to be shown after dark to be seen by enemy aircraft. The Village Hall had not yet been provided with blackout curtains. Lady Long kindly offered the Manor House as the rendezvous for hostesses and guests. It was eleven o'clock that night – a heart-rending scene – there were babies asleep on cushions on the floor, tired, worried and bewildered mothers were sitting around drinking tea, while Mrs Dixon and her helpers, with Nurse Collier, re-arranged the accommodation. Some prospective foster-mothers were less willing to take mothers and babies. They didn't all have suitable accommodation. Billets were eventually found and the weary evacuees were taken by tired hostesses to lodgings for the night and hopefully some sleep. Some necessary adjustments were made next day.

The evacuees came from Limehouse – a rather notorious slum area of London. Most of them were exceedingly poor and in the eyes of a few of the local people there were some who were pretty well uncivilized. Some of their habits came as a great shock to the clean Wiltshire country women. Babies and small children were far from being house-trained. Some of the mothers were no better. The tinies had no nappies even and knickers were unknown. Best draw a veil over some of the things that happened. The poor Londoners were not happy either and after two or three weeks of the 'phoney' war, when no bombs had fallen, many of them were relieved to return to London. Whether or not they survived the later blitzes or whether they were evacuated elsewhere later in the war when the 'doodle-bugs' and V bombs came we never knew. One or two young families remained and were joined in 1940, after Dunkirk, by some schoolchildren evacuees who attended Steeple Ashton School. A few stayed on after the war – they were more 'Turmut hoers' than cockneys by then and they made their homes in West Wiltshire, although not in the village, as they were found council houses in the neighbourhood.

THE OLDER GENERATION – THE FORGET-ME-NOTS

When, in the late 1950s, 'Super Mac' – Prime Minister Harold MacMillan – told a bemused nation, 'You never had it so good' he was not very far from the truth, at least as far as the poorer people were concerned. At that time the rigours of war-time Britain were a fast-fading memory. Food rationing, clothes rationing and shortages were no longer a necessary feature of our times. There were new homes, new schools, new roads, new almost everything and business was booming. Prospects were very bright indeed.

As a result of war-time rationing people were healthier and fitter than ever before, with a better understanding of nutrition and health. Women, who had been forced by circumstances to bring up their children single-handed and to go out to work, had discovered a resilience and independence which made them eager to preserve these assets and to widen their horizons beyond hearth and home. The proliferation of labour-saving devices for use in the home, which their more affluent status allowed them to purchase, permitted them more time to pursue their own interests. Not only were they more confident than their mothers and grandmothers had been, they were given more opportunity to make their views heard. They made themselves heard to good effect concerning the elderly. It was no longer acceptable for the retired pensioners to sit at home, or in their children's homes, a forgotten generation. There were many exciting things to be enjoyed, as far as health permitted.

Darby and Joan clubs began to appear in towns and villages throughout the land, where the over-sixties could meet for a social hour or so. Inevitably the Darbys were out-numbered by the Joans; not only did the women live longer, they retired earlier than the men and of course their numbers included many war widows. The Women's Voluntary Services initiated and supervized many such clubs, often handily referred to as 'Sixty-plus'. This title was a little too impersonal and dismissive for individual clubs which blossomed under such titles as 'Autumn Leaves', 'Silver Threads', 'Golden Circle'. The local newspapers carried news of their meetings, luncheons, dinners and outings. The *Wiltshire Times* printed many such articles, including some about the Steeple Ashton 'Forget-me-Nots'.

The 'Forget-me-Nots' meet during the afternoon of the first and third Wednesday of each month. Sometimes they are entertained by an outside speaker, sometimes one of the members can be persuaded to give a talk, accompanied by photographs and slides. Sometimes, after a little business, they sit around and chat. They exchange news on members who are absent through sickness and read letters from former members who have left the district – in short they share in a fellowship with their contemporaries. Reminiscences of times past enliven the proceedings and happy laughter accompanies the tea and biscuits, before a game of whist or bingo. The cost of these activities is minimal, funded by a tenpenny raffle and a similar contribution for tea. An occasional coffee morning at a member's house and a jumble sale in the Village Hall provides further funding, which pays for the hire of the hall and subsidizes the cost of the coach tours.

Throughout the summer months the Village Hall is deserted for one meeting each month in favour of a coach outing, sometimes for a whole day, though in the early summer or the autumn a half day suffices. Empty seats are offered to non-members for a higher fee. Visits have been enjoyed to such favourite places as Brecon, Weymouth, Bournemouth, Exeter, the Cotswolds and other beauty spots. Shopping expeditions have been arranged to Salisbury, Swindon and Poole, all in good time for Christmas, before the shops become crowded and uncomfortable.

One fine autumn day in 1987, fortunately before the October Hurricane of that year, members made a visit to Kew Gardens to see, among other things, the newest glass-house. The return journey was made via London. For two hours they toured the city, crossing and re-crossing the Thames. The knowledgeable driver sat patiently in traffic jams, pointing out places of interest along the route. At one point a traffic warden supervised the clamping of a vehicle, illegally parked on a double yellow line and causing traffic chaos. This incident was regarded gleefully, albeit tinged with a little sympathy, by the whole coach load 'up from the country'. Altogether it was a memorable day. A trip to the seaside was tame by comparison.

In December the business of the first meeting is, of course, the Christmas Dinner, which is very much appreciated and enjoyed.

For most of the members the greatest boon of the 'Forget-me-Nots' is the afternoon meeting shared with friends, with no necessity to leave home after dark. For those unable to walk help is provided by

Manor Cottages

the volunteer car drivers who make sure no-one is left out and all are safely returned to their own homes.

Not all 'Forget-me-Nots' are elderly, many actively support not only their own club, but many other village organizations, lending helping hands to fund-raising events – manning stalls, making refreshments and washing up, in the age-old way. They do not forget, neither are they forgotten.

THE HOUSEWIFE'S LOT

There have been many changes in the life of the housewife over the past century. Life became much easier once electricity came to the village in 1932; before that it was extremely hard work for the average village lady who had no other help. Indeed, she often had to undertake extra work for other people to eke out her housekeeping money. Many took on laundering and others charring, that is housework for others.

Oil lamps and candles preceded electricity for lighting. The oil lamps had to be filled with paraffin oil, the wicks trimmed and the glass shades cleaned perfectly to give a good light and avoid a strong smell. In big houses like the Vicarage there was a room set aside into which all the lamps were brought in the mornings and set ready for taking out at dusk. There was a very strong, though not unpleasant, smell of paraffin in this room, where the boots and shoes were also brought for cleaning. Lamps with mantles, similar to the then fashionable gas lights of urban areas, gave a brighter light and also some heat.

A mahogany-framed overmantle mirror was cracked in School House in late 1929 because the Aladdin lamp has been placed too near to it when Colonel Weston called on father to ask him to undertake the work of secretary to the local branch of the British Legion. At that time there was only one other member, a Mr Light. Father agreed and remained secretary for many years, receiving a Westminster chiming clock with suitable inscription in 1939, by which time the foundations for the present Steeple Ashton and District Branch were securely laid with some one hundred members. The mirror was taken to

Mr Berrett in Purnell's, Dark Lane and the glass was cut to make two smaller mirrors with new frames made of oak taken from a repaired tithe barn. The frame of the one that remains in Steeple Ashton is still sound but, unfortunately, the glass had to be replaced in 1985. It sounds a bit like the story of the chap who had a very good hoe for many years, he'd had three new blades and two new handles! A good old country joke often heard hereabouts in past days.

Candles were taken to light the way to bed. The beds were warmed in various ways, sometimes by a copper warming pan, seen now as decorative features of olde worlde rooms. Hot cinders were placed in the bowl of the pan which was then smoothed over the bottom sheet to take off the chill. Sometimes a brick warmed in the oven was wrapped in flannel and left in the bed. Some folks had stone hot water bottles, some had aluminium bottles and later, in around 1920, there came the soft luxury of cuddly hot water bottles made of rubber. These

A cottage bedroom

had another advantage, they did not burn so much when hot or get as cold or make such a noise or break when accidentally kicked out of bed! Since 1960 electric blankets, either under or over, have become popular and continental quilts or duvets have replaced the pile of blankets used in the cold houses of times past. Only the rich could enjoy the luxury of a bedroom fire; now warm radiators bring comfort on icy mornings and as houses are insulated as they never were before rooms are much warmer. Electric heaters and central heating make far less work than coal fires. Damp proof courses are non-existent in many of the old houses but special treatments are available to render them dry. The stone foundations of many of the older houses and thatched cottages can now be treated to keep out the wet and rising damp. The stone for these foundations was quarried locally, either in Quarries or Quarrel by the Lime Kiln on Raydown, or the Bratton and Edington Road, or from Windmill Field, the highest point of land between the village and Ashton Common, off Mudmead Lane near where it becomes Lyneham Way on the old maps. The dumping of rubbish for the in-filling of this quarry began in 1927. This was a favourite playground for the bigger boys in the 1920s.

It was not unusual to have to break the ice, even in the bedroom wash basin, to get water to wash on a cold winter's morning. The outdoor 'privvy' made the little receptacle under the bed a real necessity.

Coal fires, now with the luxury of smokeless fuel, were then the only form of heating and had to be kindled early before a kettle was boiled for morning tea and breakfast. Its much easier with a 'Teasmade' or an electric kettle today. A fire that wouldn't draw not only filled the house with smoke and smuts, it meant a very poor lookout at mealtimes as well as a cold house. Ashes had to be taken out and coal and wood brought in. Coal usually came in large lumps which were hard work to break into manageable pieces. Firegrates and stoves had to be cleaned with brush and blacklead and fire-irons and fenders had to be polished. If these were made of brass they gave a cheerful glow but required a liberal application of elbow grease to keep them clean.

Wash days were heavy work, especially when it was wet. There were no automatic washing machines and tumble-driers to do the work at the flick of a switch. The more fortunate homes had a copper wash-boiler in the scullery. A fire was lit under the copper, which was filled with water, carried from tap or pump at the well. Often the zinc bath used for children's bath time was used for washing the clothes which were placed on a board, often of corrugated zinc, and then rubbed or scrubbed with hard yellow soap and brush and another liberal application of 'elbow grease' – quite an arm-aching job. Some women used 'dollies' or possers or poshers. The dollies looked like three legged stools on long handles. We had a posser or posher, a basin-shaped copper tool of double thickness with holes for the water to come through; this too was on a long handle. The clothes were dollied or poshed by being pushed into the soapy water, lifted and swirled round, pushed again to force the soapsuds through. The soapsuds were made by first softening the hard water by dissolving a good handful or two of soda and adding shredded hard yellow soap to very hot water; later soap powders such as Rinso and Persil were introduced in place of the hard soap. There were washing machines in around 1930 which had a paddle fixed under the lid connected to a handle which was turned to agitate the clothes. These square machines also had a tap to draw off the water. This was considered a lazy woman's way to wash! After the Second World War electric wash boilers were to replace the copper ones in which the whites were boiled before being transferred to a bath of cold water for rinsing. The clothes were wrung out by hand unless the lucky lady had a mangle or wringer. The clothes were rinsed again in more cold water and finally in 'blue' water. A dolly or muslin-wrapped cube of 'blue' was swirled in the final rinsing water because, as the advertisements said: 'Out of the blue comes the Whitest Wash!' We learnt at school the scientific rules of blue enhancing white. Again the washing had to be wrung out or mangled, unless starching was required to stiffen the fabric. Starch prevented the dirt from penetrating and dirt and starch washed out together. Also a fine sheen was obtained when a starched article was ironed. The starch was prepared from a white powder and water in the way that powdered custards are made, mixing it with cold and then pour on boiling

water, and stirring until it turned. Men's shirt collars, which were separate from shirts, were starched first, followed by tablecloths and aprons. The starch was thinned for dresses, pillow cases and things which needed little stiffening. Starched items were gently squeezed before being hung out to dry – not in strong winds. They were really drip-dried and brought in while damp to be rolled up before being ironed with a very hot iron. Care was needed in the preparation of the starch to get the correct consistency. Too much made things too stiff and very uncomfortable to wear and too little, especially for men's collars, was wasteful and useless.

Hanging out the washing was a pleasant job on a nice sunny and breezy day but it was a misery on a cold rough day and worse still when the rain came down and the washing had to be dried on a wooden clothes horse by the fire or on the ceiling rack, hoisted up by pulley. The house filled with steam – a positive nightmare in a small house with a large family.

After all this labour came the ironing, with flat irons being heated on a trivet in front of the fire, tested for the correct temperature, often by being held in front of the face – rather dangerous – or a quick spit which dried rapidly when the correct heat was achieved. A quick rub with a cloth to make sure it was clean, maybe a patent shiny metal shield was fixed to protect the clothes from possible smuts and then press away until the iron cooled and hopefully the clothes were dry enough to be aired. What a contrast with the methods of today, when people wear fewer clothes because their houses are warmer, but the clothes are made of minimum iron and easy care materials. Detergents in the modern washing machines make light work of today's laundry and there is very little call for starch and none for the blue-bag, which by the way was a useful thing to have in case of bee stings. 'Vinegar for vasps and blue bag for bees', they said!

Keeping clean was hard work and the routine for a week's work began on Monday with washing, Tuesday ironing, Wednesday clean the bedrooms, Thursday clean the downstairs rooms extra well, Friday do the shopping and on Saturdays make cakes and pastries for the week and if you were lucky take the afternoon off. On Sunday the family sat down to mid-day dinner together and that was a special meal – sometimes it was the only day that there was meat for the poorer families. In between there was mending to be done and often clothes to be made.

In better-off families the lucky housewife had a carpet sweeper or even a vacuum cleaner. The first vacuum cleaners were operated like a treadle sewing machine and required two operators, one to pedal and the other to manipulate the suction tube. Today's cleaners are much more efficient and far cleaner than the old dust pan and brush methods or the carpet beaters required in great-grandma's day, that is always supposing she had a carpet. Most homes had rugs to be taken up and shaken outside before being replaced after the floor had been swept and possibly the surrounds polished. Some floors had to be scrubbed frequently. Many rugs were hand-made from material obtained from discarded clothing or left over from dressmaking. These were pegged or prodded. When I lived in County Durham in 1942 rug-making parties were quite the thing. The lady of the house collected her materials – swops were desirable – she found some hessian, or maybe an old sack, fitted it to a large frame and invited her neighbours in. They arrived with their poggers of pointed wood about the size of a thick fountain pen and comfortable to the hand. Three or four ladies round a frame made short work of a new rug. Usually it took about four days. They were rewarded with suitable refreshments and exchanged the news of the day. The party re-assembled next morning and the rug was fetched out again and with luck it was ready to be put down on Saturday after the cleaning was done. The lady repaid her neighbours' kindness in like manner at a later date. I have not met with this custom in Wiltshire, but I have seen many such hooky rugs. One style which seemed to be a favourite was made from old stockings – lisle, silk or better still the nylons which came over with the Americans. These were dyed, then fitted to the hessian with a continuous stitch and a tool like a crochet hook. Care had to be taken or the work unravelled very easily before it was secured. Sometimes the older children would be called upon to assist. Many a fine tale was told and much gossip exchanged while the work proceeded!

Families of eight or ten children were commonplace before 1920 and mothers of large families worked exceedingly long hours to feed and clothe them, often staying up until two in the morning so that a child could have a decent dress or pair of trousers to wear to school next day. Mother made the clothes and then she had to be up very early next morning to get breakfast for her husband and perhaps an older son – sometimes they started work at six. As they grew up the older children had to help with the work and care for the younger ones.

I remember being much impressed by the starched white pinafores, with tucks, gathers and ruffles, which many of my contemporaries wore over their woollen dresses. A lot of work for mother there! The girls often wore their long hair in ringlets, curled over rags, I think, so that was an extra job for mother, but the girls looked attractive.

The men worked hard too. Most of them were classed as farm labourers. This was a rather derogatory term, for they were skilled in their occupations and had to work long hours to obtain a living wage. Thirty-two shillings and sixpence was the basic wage for a man who worked forty-eight or even fifty-six hours a week. Overtime was paid when extra long hours were worked, such as at harvest or hay-making. The decimal equivalent would be one pound, sixty-two

The Sanctuary, Dark Lane

and a half pence. Even allowing for inflation it was a poor wage. The hours were long and arduous and didn't leave much time for gardening. Holidays were restricted to Sundays and Bank Holidays.

The large gardens of the cottages were necessary in order to grow sufficient vegetables to feed the families. Although the husband dug the garden and maybe planted it, his wife had her part to play in feeding the fowls and boiling the swill of left-overs to which barley meal was added for feeding the pigs. If there was a little ground to spare she might manage to grow a few flowers, a rose or some honeysuckle or jasmine against a wall.

Our village shops today have deliveries of fresh fruit and vegetables almost every day with salads of all kinds. Their deep freeze cabinets are stocked with frozen fish, meat, fruits and vegetables. Many families have their own freezers and refrigerators stocked with home-grown produce or stocks bought from deep-freeze centres. We live in a luxury undreamed of even twenty years ago. Fresh fish is a real luxury and we hope the present supplier will be able to maintain his weekly deliveries. Fried fish and chips are brought to the village and cooked on the spot in a modern van on Tuesday evenings. The fish and chip man with his bell was a feature of the 1930s – another treat temporarily brought to an end by the war.

The village shops have stocked most of the necessities of life over the years and they have had competition from visiting salesmen who have come with vans to sell from door to door. Some, like Mr Austin, the butcher, used horse-drawn vehicles, but by 1929 motor vans were in common use. The Porters and Holloways from Trowbridge sold paraffin oil, soap, soda, starch, clothes pegs and lines; parts for primus stoves and all kinds of kitchen hardware and mats and linoleum. Fares of Hilperton, Trowbridge Co-operative Society and Mr Sidney Berrett of Edington, who had been apprenticed to Mr Winslow, a baker of Steeple Ashton, all sold bread and cakes. In competition with Mr Austin was Trowbridge Co-op Butchery Department, Clevelands and Garlicks of Trowbridge. There was some rivalry between the salesmen and prices were keen but when people owned cars and could go out shopping in the local towns the van sales declined and deliveries stopped. The last people to deliver door-to-door were the Berretts of Edington in around 1980.

The 'Tally men' were the other regular callers, coming fortnightly, hence the nickname 'Johnny Fortnight', to sell clothes on the 'never-never' as credit sales were generally called. Mr Godbold and later Mr Martin of Trowbridge and representatives of the old firm of Slopers of Devizes were the regulars who visited customers bringing linen and clothing for all the family and collecting payment by instalments.

Mail order clubs were organized in the early days of the WI and the system was this: twenty people formed a club paying one shilling per member per week to an agent who kept the book. Lots were drawn and numbers given. The payments for one week purchased the item, usually of clothing, chosen by customer number one. The person who had drawn number twenty had paid for her goods before she received them. All items cost one pound and there were twenty shillings to one pound when these clubs were most popular between the wars. Clothing was the main item in the catalogues then but household linen, tea sets and similar articles were also available. Mail order catalogue sales are no longer organized on such rigid lines, they have a far wider and more extensive range of goods to sell and agents are not necessary. The earlier system provided a little extra for the housewife agent and the bonus she earned was more valuable when taken in goods rather than cash.

CHANGING TIMES – AMUSEMENTS

Work was harder and working hours longer but the pressures were different. The pace was slower and there was much less noise and bustle. There was time for a joke and one could stroll down the road without having to dash to cross risking life and limb from fast cars and huge, extra long lorries, with enormous wheels.

Life was not all work even then. Choir and Sunday school outings have been part of village life for as long as anyone can remember. Until the late 1920s a trip in a horse-drawn wagonette to the Monastery Gardens at Edington for a picnic tea was a great treat. The charabancs were far slower and less comfortable than the coaches of today, after all they had solid tyres and hard bench seats, but outings to the seaside were very much enjoyed. There was a trip to Burnham-on-Sea in 1926. In later years most choir outings were to Weymouth because there was always something to amuse the children if the weather was inclement. Coaches were hired from Chandler's Red Rambler of North Bradley, the same coaches that take the children to Clarendon School.

They always requested that Mr Ron Smith should be the driver. Ron was born in Vine Cottage and like his father Albert of Dark Lane he had driven the lorries of Geo. T. Brown. Albert had driven a milk lorry to Manchester in the General Strike of 1926; not a very pleasant job at all. Sadly Ron died in 1986.

Saturday afternoons in the 1950s had a special ritual for many families. The buses were crowded when father went to the football match in Trowbridge and mother and children went round the shops, to look, if not to buy. Sometimes they went to the cinema. There were then three cinemas in Trowbridge, The Gaumont where Knee's shop is now at the top of Red Hat Lane; The Regal in Bythesea Road, now a crisp factory and the New Kinema, which is now an estate agents in Bythesea Road. Mr Andrews junior, of the New Kinema used to give picture shows in the Village Hall, usually on Thursday evenings. The entry price was sixpence and the films were much enjoyed in spite of the hard chairs. In the early days people went to the 'flicks' – the pictures flickered!

The most exciting day of the year in the early 1930s was Easter Monday when the point-to-point races were held at Hag Hill or the fields behind the Church. This was the only day of the year when doors were locked in Steeple Ashton. Everyone went to the races and some of the strangers got drunk and were not to be trusted. The war changed things.

'Head in bucket, feet in sack, Watch me jump from the horse's back,' said that exciting acrobat of Tom Fossett's Circus which came to Farm Piece in 1930. A very exciting event. Such visits were rare and the animals and side-shows quite a novelty.

Pastimes that have attracted young and old spectators, if not participants, have been the New Year's Day meet of the Foot Beagles, now from the School of Infantry, Warminster. For half an hour or so before lunch a crowd gathers outside the Long's Arms to watch the dogs and hunt followers. When the dogs move off some of the spectators move with them to follow across the fields for the afternoon; some move into the inn for a warming drink and cheery chat while the rest go off for a late lunch.

The meets of the Avon Vale Foxhounds in November and March, either outside the Long's Arms or more latterly at Church Farm, attract large crowds from the village and from the surrounding countryside. Some follow the hounds, as nearly as they can, by car, some on foot or on bicycles. The official followers, members of the hunt, ride on horses of various pedigrees or ponies. They make a picturesque scene, with men in Hunting Pink, some, up until recent years, wearing the top hat or bowler, but mostly now they wear the riding caps of black velvet. The riding hats are firm crash helmets. Very few ladies now wear the bowler with the coarse veil and skirt and apron needed to ride side-saddle. After a stirrup cup the huntsman sounds his horn and the crowd moves off. They don't seem to be unduly bothered by the weather and arrive home some hours later, tired, wet, muddy but normally happy. Occasionally a dog gets lost and can be seen wandering along the lanes, until it is found and returned safely to its companions at the kennels at Spye Park. Sometimes a local farmer will take a hound puppy for training, 'puppy walking', and then attend a puppy judging to show how well they have trained their puppy, and to enjoy a social afternoon.

Business conference!

Charters, Markets and Fairs

King Edgar inherited the Manor At Aystone when he came to the throne in 959 AD. He set out its bounds in the Charter of 964, saying that he should enjoy it for his life-time and leave it to whom he wished. He eventually left it for the endowment of the Nunnery of Romsey which he re-established in 967. Some three hundred years later his successor King Henry III granted a Charter to the Abbess and Nuns of Romsey authorizing a weekly market on Wednesday at the Manor of Assheton in the county of Wiltshire and a yearly fair on the Vigil, Feast and Morrow of the Nativity of St Mary (7, 8 and 9 September). This Charter was granted at Kennylleworth, dated 18 July 1266, the fiftieth year of his reign.

In 1349 this Charter was confirmed by King Edward III to Isabella Chonnoys (or de Chameys), Abbess of Romsey, and to her heirs and successors for ever. The principal products for sale were wool, sheep, cheese, pigs, wheat and apples. Steeple Ashton remained famous for its cheese until the 1914–18 war and pigs continued to be a prominent part of the economy until at least the late 1960s. Sheep, wheat and apples are still to be found in the parish.

The greens which bordered the High Street have been eroded and some parts incorporated into the gardens of the houses on the north-east side of the road. The road itself has been widened to take heavier traffic. The old greens provided ample space for markets and fairs. In his itinerary *c.* 1540–6 John Leyland,

Antiquary to Henry VIII, remarked that out of the ashes (of the fire of 1503) of Steeple Ashton market the market at Lavington had prospered. Coincidentally in 1268 a certain Richard de la Rokele had complained that the market at Market Lavington had suffered because of the abbess's market at Church (Steeple) Ashton. It is recorded in the Victoria County History that 'the abbess blandly replied that she had no vill of that name, and the charter was confirmed by several kings, the last known confirmation being in 1537'.

In the early eighteenth century our market further declined and attempts were made to revive it in 1756 for the sale of all sorts of corn, grain, cattle, meat, all sorts of provisions and marketable wares. Again in 1766 a further attempt was made to rally the trade, but in spite of assurance that the roads to Steeple Ashton had been repaired the market failed to prosper.

The fair, which seems to have been more successful than the weekly market, was suspended in 1625, to prevent the spread of the plague. In 1770 it was held on 2 September for the sale of cheese. From 1831 it was held on 18 September, a day before Devizes Fair – a tradition which survives in Devizes to this day, with funfairs on the Green at Southbroom on 19 April and 19 September. Ashton folk have always attended, especially when the horse sales took place.

A lady who had been a servant at Ashton House told me how she and her fellow servants would go up to the roof of the house and look over the parapet to see The Green crowded with stalls, all lit by flares. These well-patronized events were looked forward to with happy anticipation. All the fun of the fair was to be enjoyed with money to spend – a shilling went a long way then. There is a story told of one who lost his shilling in the drain by The Green, outside the Rose and Crown. He took up the drain and joyfully retrieved it. I don't know whether the sideshows equalled those at Devizes, but they were much enjoyed until sadly, by the 1914–18 war, Ashton Fair ceased to be and was never seriously revived.

However, to celebrate European Architectural Heritage Year in 1975 a 'medieval fair' was arranged. Stalls were set up on the long Green in front of the Merchant's Hall; Lord Long's daughter, Sarah, set up as a fortune teller in a house on The Green, next to the Chapel House. There was a procession from Newleaze, led by two goats since sheep were not amenable to leading a procession. Small boys in 'Lincoln Green' with Robin Hood bows and arrows followed their mob-capped mothers among the 'Villeins and Yeomen' and fine feathered ladies. The White Horse Morris Men came with their music and entertained a large crowd. Traffic had to give way to the fair on that day. There were Mummers and Puppet Shows and a demonstration of farriery which drew a crowd of fascinated onlookers. The home movies of these events provided further entertainment in the Village Hall during the winter and the children were delighted to watch themselves dancing round the Maypole, among other attractions. There was a similar Fair in 1976, but unfortunately Trowbridge Carnival Committee arranged events for that same Saturday to precede their Carnival week and we lost support for further fairs. Now, instead of a fair on our traditional Feast Day the Church Social Committee arranges a Flower Festival with a Saturday Fair, approximately every third year and very successful they have been.

In 1983 the Festival replaced the more usual garden fête. The church itself was most beautifully decorated by ladies of the Melksham District Flower Arrangers Club. A cheese and wine evening at the Manor brought many visitors for a preview on Thursday evening. Visitors came from far and wide to see the flowers on following days when they visited the arts and crafts exhibition in the Village Hall and a local history exhibition in the Braziers' house in The Butts. They visited local gardens opened for the occasion and enjoyed teas especially provided.

Six stalls were set up on the village greens and did much business on the Saturday afternoon. The Morris Men and Steeple Ashton Dancers entertained the visitors and the band played on. The young people enjoyed a barbecue-disco at the rear of the Long's Arms in the evening and Sunday's festive services were well attended and enjoyed.

By the end of the year tentative plans were afoot to repeat the Festival in 1986. The Church Social Committee laid plans and contacted people and booked bands, etc., then co-opted more people to carry out the plans.

There was a most encouraging response to all the efforts made and when some plans were disorganized because of illness or other causes, fresh plans were made and substitutes were quickly forthcoming. Coffee mornings prior to the festival raised some hundreds of pounds to provide the flowers.

The Doxology Singing Group and Friends arranged an old time variety show which, by popular demand, ran for two evenings, starting the festivities a day earlier than intended and revealing a great deal of unsuspected talent among the populace. It gave an hilarious start to the week's festivities.

When our 'opener' Lord Long was prevented from coming at the last minute the local MP, Mr Denis Walters, happily deputized – with the local Parish Council Chairman, Ivor Smith supporting in his Thespian role of 'Turmut Hoer with a degree in muck spreading'.

The Lord Bishop of Salisbury was ill and Canon Richard Askew came to preach at Festival Evensong. On Monday evening a packed church enjoyed the singing of the cathedral choir and then retired to the Village Hall for coffee, cakes and a grand draw. The addresses of the lucky winners gave an indication of the wide area covered by our festival publicity. People came from beyond Bristol, Gloucestershire, Oxford, Somerset and all parts of Wiltshire, many saying that they had heard of us from the press, from GWR Radio or Radio Bristol. They had especially enjoyed BBC Radio Bristol's 'Compass' programme.

We had certainly enjoyed making that programme with Pat Pryor who had come, by arrangement, with her recording equipment one Wednesday afternoon. My daughter Mrs Rosemary Brett, Clerk to the Parish Council, Mr Doug Barnett, Steward of the Methodist Church, and I accompanied Pat around the village, first stopping on The Green to recall the history evoked by the Market Cross and Blind House and surrounding houses. We visited the blacksmith's shop which she found fascinating and as we were about to leave she recorded Ivor singing that good old Wiltshire song 'The Vly be on the Turmut', with which the programme was eventually introduced. The song has been used on Radio Bristol once or twice since.

We walked down to Silver Street to meet Tim Brown of the family firm of Geo. T. Brown, Hay & Straw Merchants, established in 1872. Bill Burbidge spoke of his schooldays and more than sixty-five years of rural life. Doug Barnett told the story of the Miracle of the non-sale of the Chapel.

George Moore's vegetable garden impressed her almost as much as his talk on the church from the point of view of a caring churchwarden and former tower-master and bell ringer – the position now held by his son Michael.

The Bullen Hill Smith brothers, Godfrey and Michael, proudly agreed that they gave a daily service, including Christmas Day, and that in addition to delivering milk and other dairy products they also acted as messengers and delivered leaflets appertaining to village events. They were on occasions called to assist ladies in distress who had inadvertently locked themselves out of their homes – got stuck in windows or were enveloped by washing when clothes-lines had broken! A recording of the church bells brought the broadcast to a close. It aroused great interest and was a faithful record of a very happy afternoon which certainly put Steeple Ashton on the map; as Pat explained to Roger Bennett, 'find Melksham on the map and then take the road to Westbury until you see the road to Steeple Ashton going off to the left!'

ROYAL OCCASIONS

Other occasions which bring back happy memories when the spirit of Steeple Ashton has been evident were the Silver Jubilees, Coronations and Royal Weddings. The Silver Jubilee of King George V and his Queen Mary in 1935 was when we saw our mothers revealing their knees (most shocking) when they ran with enthusiasm the 'Mothers Race'. The Coronation celebrations for King George VI and Queen Elizabeth were held in the field behind the Vicarage where the remains of the Deer Leap, that ancient boundary with Keevil, were still to be found. The celebrations of the Coronation of their daughter, Queen Elizabeth II were held in the same field in like manner. Her Majesty's Silver Jubilee in 1977 was celebrated first by the Long's Arms with a pig roasting – much laughter and music from a giant 'hurdy-gurdy'. Later on that day there were street parties in various venues. Red, white and blue, as always, was the theme of the day, with decorated houses and streamers across the streets. Mrs Bruges MBE was happy to tell the story of her 'Visit to Fairyland' when she received her Decoration from Queen Elizabeth the Queen Mother.

Miss Marjorie Bartlett also was honoured to receive the Queen's Silver

Jubilee Medal and Certificate to mark her long service to Steeple Ashton School as caretaker.

On each occasion the children were given mugs to commemorate the occasion just as their parents, grandparents and great-grandparents had been since Victorian times. Earlier generations had received 'Medals', the younger ones of recent years received Crowns (five shilling pieces) for the Queen's Coronation and Silver Jubilee. There were sports for all, followed by tea for the children and the old age pensioners. Earlier generations were given Raspberry Tea and Seedy Cake. Later generations enjoyed tea or squash with trifles, sandwiches and a variety of cakes. Whatever it was they received was undoubtedly a treat to remember, as well as a mug and Crown to treasure!

The Royal Weddings were not celebrated to such an elaborate degree. Nevertheless the occasions did not pass uncelebrated. There were more informal barbecues arranged in the sports field. The money for these events came partly from the Parish Council and partly from public subscriptions. The celebrations to mark the last Royal Wedding, that of the Duke and Duchess of York, were partly funded from the money given by the Council for the Protection of Rural England (CPRE) in 1984 when they awarded to Steeple Ashton the 'Best Kept Large Village Award' of the CPRE's Silver Jubilee, which meant that the village was adjudged the best of all the villages which had won the award in the previous twenty-four years. They competed in a separate class for the Jubilee Award *and we won*!

'We always expect good things of Steeple Ashton!' said Mrs Mary Pearce, Chairman of West Wiltshire District Council, when she presented the framed certificate to the Parish Council Chairman, Mr Ivor Smith, in 1985.

Steeple Ashton lives up to those expectations and has good cause to be proud of itself. In October 1984 it entertained members of the CPRE when Sir Roland Gibbs attended a ceremony on the long Green to present the award for the Best Kept of all the Best Kept Large Villages of Wiltshire for twenty-five years. In that time Steeple Ashton had won the awards for 1969, 1970, 1976, 1981 and come second in 1980. It is thought by many to be the perfect example of a Wiltshire Village. It has almost everything and jealously guards its heritage, being proud of its history.